Becoming Maria Kim:
The Versions I Had to Bury

by Maria Kim

Becoming Maria Kim

ISBN: 978-1-965951-41-5 (sc)

Seraphim Global Media LLC 155 Willow brook Blvd Ste 110
Wayne, NJ 07470
+1 888-347-1877
fullfillment@seraphimgml.com

Becoming Maria Kim
DEDICATION

For the little version of me
who learned how to be strong
before she ever learned how to be loved.

For every child who grew up feeling too different,
too poor,
too loud,
or never enough —
this story is for you.

For my Mama and Papa,
for Florame and Kevin,
for the family who shaped my roots
before the world ever knew my name.

For my husband, Marcus —
who chose me when I was still learning how to choose myself,
who loved me without conditions,
and who stands beside me as proof
that real love still exists.

For every LGBTQ+ soul
who had to fight just to exist,
to become,
to love out loud.

And finally…
for Maria Kim —
the woman I became
after surviving everything that tried to break me.

AUTHOR'S NOTE

I wrote this book not because my life was perfect—but because it was not.

This story is my truth as I remember it. Some names were changed. Some details were protected. But the emotions—those are real.

This book is for everyone who felt different, broken, rejected, or lost. If this story gave you even a small spark of hope, then every pain I lived through had meaning.

With all my truth,
Maria Kim

TABLE OF CONTENTS

CHAPTER ONE:

THE CHILD BORN IN A STORM

I was born during Bagyong Ruping—
a storm so strong it ripped off rooftops, flooded entire barangays,
and turned our town into a scene you'd expect from an end-of-the-
world movie.

My mother used to joke that I didn't cry like a baby —
I cried like the storm.
Loud. Dramatic.
Parang may audition sa teleserye na wala pa ko kabalo.

Maybe that was the universe's first warning:
"This child will not live a quiet life."

We were extremely poor.
Not "tight budget" poor —
but the kind of poor where every day felt like a question:
"Makakain ba tayo ngayon?"

My parents sold trays of eggs in the market.
That was our livelihood, our routine, our survival.
I grew up in a squatter area where children ran barefoot,
neighbors shouted from window to window,
and the street smelled like a mix of cooking oil, dust, and tsismis.

It was chaotic, messy, loud.
But it was also home.

Outside, life was fun and unpredictable.
Inside, life was... complicated.

Becoming Maria Kim

My father was the strictest man I knew.
His footsteps alone could erase a smile from my face.
He believed in discipline the way other fathers believed in affection.
His rules were simple:

"Boys should act like boys."
And whatever I was,
it wasn't the kind of "boy" he approved of.

I moved with softness even before I understood what softness
meant.
A tilt of my wrist,
a swing of my hips,
a spark in my eyes —
all of it triggered something in him.

One wrong move and the belt came out.
Another wrong move, the hanger.
Another day, just his bare hands.
He didn't shout often,
but his silence was scarier.

I learned to live with constant fear —
the kind you hide with a forced smile.

But the worst memory came unexpectedly.

One day, I was in the living room,
sashaying like a Miss Universe candidate,
pretending the floor was a runway and the world was finally
cheering for me.

I remember hearing the clapping from the TV,
the music,
the confidence of the contestants.

For a moment, I felt free.

Becoming Maria Kim

Then my father appeared.
His expression said everything.

The beating came faster than I could cry.
I remember thinking,
"Is this how I die? While pretending to be Miss Universe?"

Of course, I didn't die.
But something inside me did.

Fear replaced innocence.
Silence replaced joy.
Pretending replaced honesty.

And that was the first time I felt truly confused about love.

"If he loves me, why does it hurt this much?"
"If I'm his child, why am I the one he wants to erase?"

Thankfully, the universe balanced him out with my mother—
gentle, soft, patient,
and the only person who made me feel seen.

We were inseparable.
She took me everywhere... especially to the ladies' department store.

And that place—
that aisle full of heels, blouses, perfumes, and bags—
was my first taste of freedom.

While my mother tried on shoes,
I slipped my feet into hers whenever she wasn't looking.
The click of the heel, the way my body moved—
it felt right in a way I couldn't explain yet.

Then I'd stare at the mirror and see
a version of myself no one else knew.

But fear was always louder.

Before I could enjoy it,
I'd whisper to myself:

"Lalaki ako. Tama lang dapat."

Even though nothing inside me agreed.

And then came childhood crushes —
the confusing kind.

I had a girl best friend, Maria Carmela.
Sweet. Loyal. My partner in crime.
Sometimes I thought I liked her.
Sometimes I thought I loved her.
Most of the time, I was just trying to prove something to myself.

But then... Patrick happened.

Patrick — my classmate who looked like **Patrick Garcia** during his
Gimik prime.
Same boyish hair.
Same innocent appeal.
Same pa-cute smile na maka-kurog ug tuhod.

Whenever he talked to me,
I felt like **Desiree del Valle** in *Tabing Ilog*,
the dramatic, quiet one with a secret crush she refuses to admit.

Then came our school retreat—
a night that changed everything.

The lights were dim,
everyone was settling into their sleeping bags,
and to my shock,
Patrick chose the spot right next to me.

Becoming Maria Kim

My classmates teased me endlessly:
"Uy! Tabing Ilog moment!"
"Si Desiree del Valle oh!"
"Bayota gyud oi!"

I denied everything,
but everyone knew.
Even Patrick knew.

Before the teacher turned off the lights,
Patrick leaned in
and kissed me on the cheek.

The room exploded.
Screaming, laughing, teasing.

But all I heard was my heartbeat—
loud, uncontrollable,
like a drum inside my chest.

I couldn't sleep the whole night.

It wasn't butterflies.
It was the entire zoo —
lions, elephants, giraffes —
running around my chest.

For the first time,
I felt something completely real.
Something that wasn't fear.
Something that wasn't punishment.
Something that was mine.

But reality inside my home wasn't kind enough for that truth.

So, I buried it.

I buried my femininity.
I buried my softness.

Becoming Maria Kim

I buried the shoes I wanted to wear.
I buried the laugh I wanted to release.
I buried the crush that made me feel alive.
I buried the child I actually was.

Childhood became a graveyard of versions I wasn't allowed to keep.

But buried things don't stay buried forever.

Even under fear,
even under pain,
even under confusion…

something inside me survived —
a small, stubborn part
that whispered:

"One day… you will become who you really are."

And that—
that quiet, stubborn whisper—
was the beginning
of everything.

CHAPTER TWO:

THE SUMMER THAT BROKE ME OPEN

High school was supposed to be a fresh start.

A cleaner version of myself.

A braver version.

A version that didn't have to pretend so much anymore.

And honestly, by that time, I already knew.

I wasn't confused.

I wasn't trying to prove anything to myself.

I finally accepted what I was trying to hide since childhood:

Bayot gyud ko.

And I wasn't sorry about it.

That summer break felt like a reward—finally, no teachers, no uniforms, no pretending.

I spent most days with my best friend, until one afternoon,

she introduced me to her cousin from Manila.

Becoming Maria Kim

His name was Toper.

Slim, tan, quiet, the kind of boy who didn't know he was handsome.

The kind of boy who smiled with his eyes first before his lips.

The kind of boy who made your heartbeat skip one second, then overcompensate by racing twice as fast.

The moment I saw him, something inside me whispered,

"Ay, patay. Crush na ni."

They lived two miles away, but love—especially teenage love—doesn't care about distance.

I walked. Every day. Under the sun. With no complaint.

Para lang makakita niya.

And every time akong bestfriend muingon ug,

"Na-a si Toper karon,"

my whole body suddenly became a Disney character—

wide eyes, glowing skin, ready for romance kahit walay permiso.

That summer felt like a montage from a teen movie.

Becoming Maria Kim

We would ride his bike—me sitting behind him, arms barely
touching his back,

but feeling like our souls were already in a relationship.

Every slight turn of the bike, I held on to him a little tighter,

praying he couldn't hear how loud my heart was beating.

Sometimes we watched movies together.

Yung tipong cheap DVDs lang, sitting too close for "friends,"

laughing at the funny parts,

pretending not to glance at each other when the romantic scenes
played.

It was the kind of summer that made you believe in love too early.

Days blurred into one long, sweet memory:

bike rides, jokes, shared snacks, secret glances,

moments that felt like they were building up to something.

I fell.

Hard.

Silently.

Surely.

Becoming Maria Kim

And just when I thought life was giving me a small taste of happiness…

Summer ended.

"Uli nako Manila," he said one afternoon.

My chest tightened.

I felt it—the familiar sting, the warning sign.

The story was about to turn.

I knew I had only one chance left.

Only one moment before he disappeared from my life forever.

So I gathered every piece of courage I had been collecting since childhood—

all the fear, all the softness, all the hidden parts of me—

and I confessed.

It wasn't dramatic at first.

Just simple words, spoken quietly.

"I like you."

He froze.

Looked at me, surprised… then uncomfortable.

"Sorry," he said softly.

"Straight man ko.

Friends ra gyud akong tan-aw nimo."

The world didn't end—

pero murag nibuto ang akong kalibutan sulod sa akong lawas.

I tried to smile, but my face betrayed me.

My throat tightened.

My vision blurred.

My heart felt like it was pulled out, wrung dry, and thrown back into my chest.

I wanted to be strong,

wanted to pretend it didn't hurt.

But when you're young,

and it's your first real confession,

your first taste of honesty,

your first leap of courage...

rejection feels like dying in slow motion.

I walked home that day with shaky legs,

trying not to cry until I reached my room.

Pag-abot nako sa balay,

I locked the door, lay on the floor,

and cried the way teenagers cry—

silent at first, then uncontrollable,

hugging my own body because no one else would.

It wasn't just heartbreak.

It was humiliation.

It was loss.

It was fear.

Fear that maybe my father was right all along.

Fear that maybe no one would ever love someone like me.

Fear that maybe being myself meant being alone forever.

That night, I learned one of the hardest lessons of my life:

Sometimes, the first love you lose

is the version of yourself you thought someone would choose.

But summer ended.

And I woke up the next morning still breathing.

Broken, yes.

Pero buhi.

And sometimes, that's enough.

THE BOY I LOVED IN SECRET

The first day of school felt like walking into a new world—
fresh notebooks, new uniforms, new faces…
and a whole hallway full of eye candy.

I enrolled in a private sectarian university for high school,
and my entire section was **all boys**.

Which means only one thing:

My inner gay awakened like Sailor Moon.
Ready.
Visible.
Alive.
But still pretending not to be obvious.

Becoming Maria Kim

I tried to hide it, of course.
But how can you hide it when everywhere you look,
there's a cute boy fixing his necktie,
another boy flipping his hair,
or someone laughing in a way na ma-refresh imong ovaries ug kalit?

Impossible.

But here's the twist—
while my heart was busy choosing crushes,
my mind was focused on something else:

Proving myself.

I knew my father would never be proud of who I was,
so I tried to give him something he *could* be proud of.

Grades.
Awards.
Achievements.

Para nako,
academic excellence became my apology
for being the child he didn't want.

So I became an achiever.
A top student.
Freshman of the year.
The kind of kid teachers adored.

I joined **BSP (Boy Scouts of the Philippines)**
because I thought maybe, just maybe,
looking "discipline" and "boyish" on the outside
could distract from the truth I was trying to hide.

But of course, the universe gave me a plot twist:

Stephen.

Becoming Maria Kim

Tall, smart, charming.
Not too handsome, but something about him just felt...
safe.
Warm.
Comfortable.

He never made me feel weird for being me.
Actually, wala gyud siya'y reklamo sa akong pagka bayot.
He treated me like a normal friend—
no malice, no judgment.

And that... was dangerous.

Because kind boys are the most dangerous for people like me.

We became best friends.
Laughing together.
Studying together.
Walking home together.

And in every moment,
I was falling deeper,
quietly, silently, desperately...

into someone who would never be mine.

I never told him.
Not because I didn't want to,
but because I knew what happens when you tell the truth:

You lose people.

And I couldn't lose him.
Not him.

So I kept everything in,
smiling like a best friend,
but loving like a secret.

Becoming Maria Kim

Then one ordinary afternoon,
while fixing my notes in class,
I overheard a group of boys talking.

"Uy, naa na si Stephen'y uyab."
"Gwapa kaayo."
"Perfect match sila."

It felt like someone punched me in the chest.

My heart dropped.
My breathing changed.
The room blurred.
My pencil slipped from my hand.

And for the first time in high school,
I felt real heartbreak—
the kind that doesn't break your bones,
but breaks your confidence.

When I got home,
I cried in silence again.
Just like childhood.
Different boy, same pain.

I hugged my pillow and whispered:
"What's wrong with me?"

Was it my face?
My voice?
My softness?
Or simply the fact that I was gay?

I was still young,
but pain makes you grow faster than age ever will.

And that day,
something shifted inside me.

I started wondering
if love was something meant for other people—
people who fit the mold,
people who weren't confusing,
people who weren't "different."

That heartbreak didn't just crack my heart.

It cracked my self-esteem.

And for the first time in my life,
I asked myself one question
that would haunt me for years:

"Will anyone ever love someone like me?"

What I didn't know was that this question—
this wound—
would follow me into adulthood,
into relationships,
into choices,
and even into the versions of myself
I would eventually bury.

THE DEAL THAT CHANGED EVERYTHING

Being an achiever saved me in ways people will never understand.

My classmates thought I studied because I loved school.
My teachers believed I was naturally gifted.
But the truth was simpler and much heavier:

I studied to survive.

Because the only thing standing between my father's acceptance
and another beating
was my report card.

One night, he called me into the living room.
For the first time in a long while,

he wasn't angry.
He wasn't shouting.

He was serious.

"Kung gusto ka nga dawaton tika," he said,
"ayaw lang ko'g pildi.
As long as you keep your grades high…
I will accept you.
Pero if mubagsak ka?
Itul-id ta ka balik. Sabtan nimo?"

Straightforward.
Cold.
Conditional.

But for someone like me—
a child who had been hiding, tiptoeing, shrinking,
praying for even a tiny sliver of acceptance—
it felt like sunlight.

I nodded.
I promised.
I told myself I could handle it.

And because I never wanted to go back to a life of hiding,
I pushed myself even harder.

I studied late.
I made honor rolls.
I competed.
I placed.
I topped exams.

Every achievement felt like a negotiation with freedom.

And true to his word,
my father started to soften.

Becoming Maria Kim

For the first time ever,
he took me shopping in the **ladies' department store**—
the same sanctuary that shaped my childhood.

I still remember the way my heart raced
when he allowed me to choose clothes.
Not loudly, not proudly,
but silently —
like a man giving permission to a secret he didn't want to talk about.

That day felt like a dream.
A moment where the world made sense for once.

And sometimes,
on rare days when courage won over fear,
I cross-dressed.

Not fully.
Not loudly.
Just little things—tops, accessories, soft colors.

The first time I did it,
I looked at myself in the mirror…
and for a moment,
I felt beautiful.

But beauty can be cruel when you're young and unsure.

Because after a few seconds,
my smile faded.

The reflection didn't feel empowering.
It felt… wrong.
Not because I hated femininity —
but because I realized something painful:

This version of me didn't look respected.
This version looked laughed at.

Mocked.
Ridiculed.

I remembered every boy who laughed at me.
Every whisper behind my back.
Every "bayot gani na"
that stung like a slap.

I stared at my reflection,
and for the first time,
instead of seeing a dream,
I saw a joke.

And I broke.

Quietly.
Slowly.
In front of a mirror.

I took off the clothes piece by piece,
folding them like they were sins,
each fold a reminder that the world was not ready for me.

And that night,
I told myself:

"Hindi ako bagay maging babae.
Maybe I am not meant to be this version."

So I stopped.

No more crossdressing.
No more soft colors.
No more little pieces of myself that made me feel alive.

I changed myself —
even if it meant killing something inside me.

Because that was the price of acceptance.
That was the deal.
That was survival.

And even though it hurt,
I chose to survive.

For now.

THE BETRAYAL THAT MADE ME A LEADER

High school wasn't just about grades, heartbreaks, or pretending I
was okay.
It was also the time I found something I never thought I'd have:

A tribe. A family. A barkada that made me feel human.

We called ourselves **The Weirdo Society**—
not because we were strange,
but because the world felt too small for kids like us.
Kids who were achievers.
Kids who dreamed too big.
Kids who didn't fit the typical teenage mold.

There was Kent—
confident, loud, the "future politician" of the group.

There was Maresheen—
smart, organized, the mother hen who brought snacks and drama.

There was you—
the overachiever with too many emotions and not enough outlets.

And the rest of the circle were just as driven, ambitious, and proudly
nerdy.

Our everyday life looked like this:

Running to the canteen during recess,
sharing baon kahit gutom ang tanan,

21

studying together during lunch,
laughing at teachers who mispronounced things,
crying over grades,
picking each other up during failures,
calling each other out sa mga crush,
and dreaming of a future na mura'g accessible ra if magkuyog mi
tanan.

Inside that circle,
I wasn't "the gay kid."
I wasn't "the soft one."
I wasn't "the one people judged."

I was simply...
one of them.

For the first time in my life,
I felt equal.

And that kind of friendship—
that kind of acceptance—
felt like air I didn't know I was suffocating without.

But high school, like life, has a way of testing the things you love.

One day, our English teacher announced a **choric speech
competition**.
It was a big deal—
40 members per team, intense rehearsals, full costumes,
and bragging rights for the entire year.

She needed student leaders.
Three of them.

And she chose **me**,
Kent, and **Maresheen**.

Becoming Maria Kim

My heart soared.
Finally, a chance to prove myself—
not as the "gay achiever,"
not as the "special child of the ladies' department,"
but as a leader.

We were told to pick our 40 members.
First come, first serve.
Kung kinsay mu-sign up, mao'y imong team.

I thought it would be simple.
I thought natural ra nga matunga ang barkada.
I thought friendship worked like that.

But when the sign-up sheets were released…

Every single one of them
walked toward Kent and Maresheen.

Not one—
not a single one—
chose to be part of mine.

I stood there holding my empty paper
while the two of them filled theirs within minutes.

They laughed,
excited,
busy organizing their teams…

and I stood alone
in the middle of a noisy classroom
that suddenly felt too quiet.

My throat tightened.
My hands went cold.
The noise blurred into a muffled hum,
like the world muted itself just to let the heartbreak echo louder.

Becoming Maria Kim

And inside me
a familiar question rose from my childhood wounds:

"What's wrong with me?"
"Am I really that easy to leave behind?"
"Di ba nila ko friend?"

It wasn't jealousy.
It wasn't competition.
It was abandonment—
the kind that doesn't scream,
but slices quietly.

I felt invisible.
Unworthy.
Replaceable.

I wondered if my sexuality made me the least appealing leader.
If my softness made me the weakest choice.
If I was only part of the group
when the situation didn't require choosing sides.

For the first time,
my achievements couldn't save me.
My grades couldn't protect me.
My smile couldn't hide the fact that my heart was breaking.

But pain—especially high school pain—
can either destroy you
or build the strongest version of you.

And that day,
I made a decision:

I will lead whoever chooses me.
Even if it's just a handful.

Even if I have to work twice as hard.
Even if no one believes I can.

So I went around the classroom,
approached classmates who barely knew me,
invited the shy ones,
the quiet ones,
the students no one thought to pick.

Slowly,
name by name,
my list grew.

We weren't the popular team.
We weren't the loudest.
We weren't the most confident.

But we showed up.
We practiced.
We worked hard.
We turned our weaknesses into something worth watching.

And on competition day...
we didn't win.
Pero we didn't embarrass ourselves either.

We performed with heart.

And that was enough.

Years later,
when I look back at that moment,
I realize something powerful:

People not choosing you
doesn't mean you're not worthy.

**Sometimes, it simply means
you're meant to lead those who don't fit anywhere else.**

That moment broke me,
yes,
but it also made me.

It taught me how to lead with empathy.
It taught me how to understand people who feel invisible.
It taught me how to stand alone
without feeling small.

And the best part?

Despite that painful chapter,
we remained friends.
We grew.
We matured.
We graduated with honors.
And The Weirdo Society
stayed a part of my life—
older, wiser,
less childish,
and more loving.

We laugh about it now.
We talk about how childish we were.
We tease each other about the sign-up sheets and the "accidental
betrayal."

But back then...
it was the wound that taught me self-worth.

And like every wound in my life,
it didn't kill me.
It carved me.

It turned me from a soft-spoken achiever
into a leader with a spine.

Becoming Maria Kim

A leader who learned the hard way:
Not everyone who loves you will choose you.
But those who don't choose you
can still stay in your story.

And with that,
high school ended—
beautiful, brutal, heartbreaking,
and unforgettable.

I walked into graduation day with medals,
a few hidden scars,
and a heart that still hoped for love...

but stronger now,
ready for whatever version of myself
I would have to bury next.

CHAPTER THREE:

THE WORLD WASN'T READY, BUT I WENT ANYWAY

Graduation from high school felt like stepping out of one battle and straight into another.
No more uniforms, no more assignments, no more teenage drama...
pero mas grabe ang reality nga akong giatubang.

My father sat me down one night with a tone that felt like a verdict.

"Kung dili ka makapasar sa Cebu Normal University,"
he said,
"dili ka mo–college."

No extensions.
No options.
No second chances.

It hurt, knowing my dreams depended on one exam and not on their support.
But that was my life.
Love was always conditional.
Acceptance was always negotiated.
And the only thing I could control was my determination.

So I studied.
Hard.
Harder than I had ever studied in my life.

While other teenagers were out celebrating, resting, or enjoying their freedom,
I was in my room memorizing concepts, answering reviewers,
praying quietly to every saint I could remember.

The day of the entrance exam felt like judgment day.
My hands were shaking.
My heart was loud.
My mind was screaming:

"This decides everything."

When the results came out...
I passed.

Not just passed.
I passed with pride —
enough to secure my place in Cebu Normal University,
a school known for producing the country's top teachers.

For the first time in a long time,
I saw pride in my parents' eyes.

I entered college with one thing clear in my heart:

Teaching was my calling.
Even as a child,
I pretended to be a teacher to imaginary students.
I corrected my siblings' grammar.
I explained lessons to my classmates even when I barely understood
them myself.

It wasn't a fallback.
It wasn't a forced choice.
It was destiny.

So I enrolled in the Education Department,
major in Special Education —
because I wanted to teach children who needed more patience,
more understanding,
more love.
The kind of love I rarely received growing up.

But college wasn't easy.

Becoming Maria Kim

We were poor,
and "poor student life" hit differently when your parents literally
couldn't afford your future.

So I fought hard.
I became a **consistent Dean's Lister**.
I studied every night.
I maintained my grades because my life depended on it.

But beyond that,
I hustled.

I had **sidelines** everywhere,
doing anything that allowed me to earn even a small amount:

- I made projects for classmates who were too lazy
- I became a tutor for kids in the neighborhood
- I choreographed school performances
- I organized events — birthdays, contests, programs, anything
- I joined academic competitions for prize money
- I even wrote essays for students in other departments

Every peso I earned had a purpose:
tuition, photocopies of handouts, travel fare, baon.

There were days I only had enough money for one meal.
Days when I walked to school because jeepney fare was too
expensive.
Days when I cried quietly knowing how hard life was...
but still woke up determined the next day.

Because despite everything —
the exhaustion, the pressure, the hunger, the uncertainty —
I was happy.

I was building something.
I was shaping my own future.
I was becoming someone no one expected me to be.

Becoming Maria Kim

For the first time,
I wasn't surviving for acceptance.
I was thriving for myself.

This chapter of my life was difficult,
messy,
tiring,
but proud.

I was becoming stronger.
More independent.
More resilient.
More certain of who I was and where I wanted to go.

But what I didn't know then
was that college…
would bring new wounds,
new heartbreaks,
new versions of myself I would one day need to bury.

This was only the beginning.

THE BIRTHDAY THAT BROKE ME

College turned me into a walker.
Almost every day, naglakaw ko padulong school.
Forty-five minutes under the sun,
ten minutes under the shade,
and a lifetime under pressure.

But God gave me one gift to survive all that:

Rudy.

My neighbor, my partner in crime, and later, one of my closest
friends.
Parehas mi ug agi:

parehas bayot,
parehas pobri,
parehas fighter sa kinabuhi.

Every walk to school felt like a comedy show.
We complained, laughed, overshared,
and gossiped about things that were none of our business.
Our poverty didn't feel heavy because we carried it together.

But there was another reason I looked forward to school—
a reason I couldn't tell anyone yet.

Calvin.

Cute. Soft-spoken.
Kind smile, gentle eyes,
and the type of guy nga kung mo-smile nimo,
your knees turn into cooked spaghetti.

He was the first person I looked for every morning.
The first one who could change my whole mood with a simple "Hi."

Sometimes he walked with us.
Sometimes he rode the jeep with me.
Sometimes he sat beside me during class,
enough for my heartbeat to ruin my concentration.

He made my college life bittersweet—
bright but painful,
calming but confusing,
kilig pero sakit.

And my friends saw it all.
Stell—dramatic and loyal.
Rona—protective and loud.
They supported me every step of the way.
They hyped me up, made me feel pretty,
and always said:

"Manifestation ra na, geng. Basin naa pud siya'y feelings."

I wanted to believe them.

Then came **February 14—**
my birthday.

My family never celebrated birthdays.
No cake.
No balloons.
No surprises.
No "Happy Birthday" unless ma-remember nila.

But that year,
for the **first time in my entire life**,
my parents allowed me to celebrate.

I felt like the universe loved me for one day.
I invited my college friends.
We bought cheap drinks.
We shared pancit and biscuits.
And Calvin came.

It felt like destiny.
Valentine's Day.
My birthday.
My crush sitting across from me while the room spun with laughter.

I wasn't drunk,
but I was brave.
Braver than I should have been.

So in the middle of the celebration,
heart pounding,
hands shaking,
I confessed everything:

"I like you.
Since the day we met.
Ikaw gyud akong crush."

Silence.

Not the romantic silence.
Not the "give him time to respond" silence.

This was the silence that warns you:
prepare, something painful is coming.

Calvin hesitated.
Looked at the floor,
then slowly lifted his eyes to me.

"Sorry," he said,
"naa koy uyab."

The room froze.

"Oh... kinsa?" I asked, forcing a smile.

He pointed at one of my classmates—
someone who was RIGHT THERE,
sitting in my living room,
eating my food,
smiling like nothing was wrong.

That was when I realized:
everyone knew.
Except me.

My stomach dropped.
My face burned.
My heart cracked so loudly I swear the whole room heard it.

I felt betrayed.
Blindsided.
Humiliated.

Becoming Maria Kim

It was supposed to be my birthday.
My first birthday celebration ever.
My one chance to feel special.

Pero ngano ako pa man ang nag-heartbreak?

Why did I end up crying in a celebration meant for me?

Why did they let me confess
when they knew the truth all along?

I excused myself,
went inside my room,
locked the door,
and cried silently—
the kind of cry where you cover your mouth
so no one hears the sound of your heart collapsing.

It was Valentine's Day.
People outside were celebrating love.
Inside my room,
I was grieving a love that was never mine.

And for the first time as an adult,
I asked myself:

"Am I really that unlovable?"
"Am I the joke in someone else's story?"
"Is this what being different means?"

But heartbreak doesn't last forever.
Humiliation doesn't define you.
And pain—especially pain you don't deserve—
eventually becomes wisdom.

That night taught me:

You can give people a seat at your table
and they will still hide knives behind their back.

**You can love loudly
and be rejected quietly.**

**You can celebrate life
and still break on the happiest day of the year.**

But most importantly:

**People not choosing you
doesn't erase your worth.
It only reveals who never deserved you.**

When the tears dried,
I came out of my room,
acted like nothing happened,
and pretended I was okay—
because that's what survivors do.

But deep inside,
I promised myself:

**"One day, someone will choose me.
For now, I will choose myself first."**

It was painful,
humiliating,
and unforgettable—

but it shaped me.

And that is how
my Valentine's birthday
became the day I realized:

**Not all heartbreaks come from love.
Some come from the people who stayed silent
when they should have protected you.**

THE PAIN THAT PUSHED ME FORWARD

Walking almost every day to Cebu Normal University became my
routine—
a routine of sweat, sunburn, and survival.
But it never felt too heavy because I wasn't walking alone.

Rudy walked beside me.
My neighbor, my mirror, my fellow warrior.
Same struggles, same softness, same poverty, same dreams.
We laughed at our misery,
turned hardships into jokes,
and made the long walk feel like a runway.

And of course, there was **Calvin**,
the boy who made my college life feel like a K-drama:
sweet, slow-burn, and doomed from the beginning.
Every morning, I looked for him the moment I stepped inside the
classroom.
His smile could erase my exhaustion.
His voice could fix my day.

Then came my **Valentine's Day birthday**,
my first-ever celebration in my entire life...
which also became my first adult heartbreak.

Confession.
Rejection.
Betrayal.
Humiliation.

And yet—

That heartbreak did not destroy me.

It woke me up.

It pushed me harder.
It sharpened my focus.

Becoming Maria Kim

It reminded me that **love is not oxygen—
you won't die without it.**

So I poured every broken piece of myself into my future.

I worked.
I studied.
I hustled.
I joined every competition,
accepted every sideline job,
memorized lessons until dawn,
and walked kilometers for my dreams.

Life hit me with heartbreak—
but I hit back with achievements.

I graduated with **Latin honors—**
something no one in my family expected,
something poverty tried to stop,
something heartbreak could never steal from me.

Before I even got my teaching license,
schools were already offering me jobs.

Because pain didn't break me—
it polished me.

People started calling me "inspiring,"
as if I was some poster child of resilience.
They admired how I persevered.
How love didn't stop me.
How I pushed through heartbreaks like they were exams.

But deep inside, I knew the truth:

I was strong... because I had no choice.

And as much as I convinced myself
that I didn't need romantic love to survive,
there were nights I still wondered:

"Makaya ba gyud nako nga wala koy love life?"
"Is achievement enough to fill the empty spaces?"
"Is success enough to replace affection?"

But even if romantic love wasn't there,
another kind of love held me together—

friendship.

Not the casual kind.
Not the "hi-hello" classmates.
But the kind of friendship that saved my life:

Stell.
Rudy.
Rona.
Joyce.
Alexis.

They gave me the love I never received at home.
They celebrated my wins.
Carried me through heartbreaks.
Fed me when I had no money.
Laughed with me until my pain felt smaller.
Reminded me I was enough,
even when I didn't believe it.

It wasn't a perfect friendship—
we fought, we argued, we messed up,
but their love was real.

And for the first time in my life, I realized:

Love isn't always romantic.
Sometimes love is the friend who waits for you after class.

Becoming Maria Kim

The friend who walks beside you under the sun.
The friend who wipes your tears even when you pretend, you're
not crying.
The friend who stays when life becomes too heavy.

All my life,
I searched for acceptance from my father,
validation from crushes,
and affection from boys who didn't choose me.

But in the end,
it was my friends
who became the home I didn't know I needed.

They became my lifeline.
My safe place.
My reason to keep going.

And this is the truth I didn't expect to discover:

You don't survive because people love you.
You survive because someone, somewhere, refuses to let you
fall.

I didn't survive college because I was strong.
I survived because I was loved—
not by family,
not by crushes,
not by society—

but by the few people
who saw me,
stood by me,
and never let go.

And with my diploma in one hand,
and my wounds in the other,
I stepped out of college with one promise:

**"The world may break me again.
But this time, I'm ready."**

This was the end of my college life—
but only the beginning
of who I was about to become.

CHAPTER FOUR:

THE DAY THE WORLD SHOWED ITS TEETH

My first teaching salary was ₱9,000.

₱9,000 to survive.
₱9,000 to support a family.
₱9,000 to dream.
₱9,000 to pretend I wasn't drowning.

In a Filipino family, the day you earn is the day you begin to give.
And I gave.
Willingly, lovingly—
but with a quiet ache that whispered:

**"Kinsay muhatag nako? Kinsay mupugos sa kalibutan nga
tagaan pud ko'g gamay?"**

I taught all day.
I tutored all night.
I choreographed sidelines.
I grabbed extra work like lifelines thrown into a storm.

But no matter how hard I worked,
my wallet remained thin,
and my self-worth even thinner.

That's the thing about poverty—
it doesn't just empty your pockets.
It empties your hope.

Then came ESL.

It felt like a door finally opening,
a space where I wasn't just a teacher but a voice that mattered.

Becoming Maria Kim

I became a supervisor.
I earned trust, respect, and a version of confidence I had never tasted
before.

And then...
Shin.

Shin, with his gentle eyes and soft voice.
Shin, who asked about my day like it truly mattered.
Shin, who smiled at me in ways I had never been smiled at before.

Kindness is dangerous when you're starved of affection.
It becomes its own language.
One you read too deeply, too quickly, too desperately.

Then one night —
we were drinking, laughing, feeling lighter than usual —
and he kissed me.

A sudden, alcohol-flushed kiss.

My world lit up.
My chest cracked open.
My stupid, hopeful heart whispered:

"Finally... ako na."

But the next day, he said the words that flattened me:

"I like someone... si Apple."

Apple — my coworker.
My friend.
My subordinate.

The humiliation was quiet but sharp,
the kind that leaves marks beneath the skin.

Still, I followed them on a trip to Moalboal —
because heartbreak makes fools out of those who only know how to
love deeply.

They sat beside each other on the bus.
I sat behind them, watching the back of a man I loved lean toward a
woman he wanted.

On the shore, they walked together,
and I walked behind them—
a ghost, a shadow, a spectator in my own story.

I was the chaperone to my own heartbreak.

And that should've been enough pain for one lifetime.

But the world wasn't finished with me.

It was only showing its teeth.

My Japanese boss called for me a few days later.
I entered the room expecting a conversation.

Instead, I experienced my first public humiliation as an adult.

He grabbed me—
literally grabbed me—
by the back of my neck,
like I wasn't a teacher,
not a supervisor,
not a human being,
but something disposable.

He dragged me out of the facility
while my coworkers watched with wide, terrified eyes.

Not one person stepped in.
Not one friend.
Not one voice said:

"Ayaw ana, sir."
"Dili na tama."
"Dili siya hayop."

Fear froze them.

Fear silenced them.

Fear made them forget I ever mattered.

My boss shouted:

"You broke policy! You went out with a client!"

He pushed me out into the open hallway.
The floor felt cold beneath my knees.
My dignity scattered like broken glass.

Then the final blow:

"We will file a case against you."

A case?
Against *me*?
The one dragged, humiliated, powerless?

I had no money.
No savings.
No lawyer.
No safety net.
Just fear... and poverty... and pain.

And when I looked around,
everyone I thought would stand beside me
turned their back —

not out of cruelty,
but out of cowardice.

Sometimes, abandonment is quiet.
Sometimes, it looks like people pretending they don't see your
suffering.

I walked six miles to the lawyer who could help me.
Six miles under the scorching sun.
Six miles with no pamasahe.
Six miles with a bruised neck and a shaking spirit.

Every step felt like the world whispering:

"Tan-awa. Walay mo laban nimo."
"Tan-awa. Ana ka ka sayon hilabtan."
"Tan-awa. Ang kalibutan dili gyud para sa imo."

But I kept walking.

Because the alternative was to collapse.
And people like me aren't allowed to collapse.

We walk.
We endure.
We survive.

When I reached the house, the lawyer listened.
She believed me.
She defended me.

The case was dropped.
The nightmare ended.

But something inside me stayed shattered.

That day, I realized something painful and true:

**The world shows its teeth first
to those it assumes cannot bite back.**

And that was the day I made myself a promise:

**One day, I will grow my own teeth.
Sharper.
Stronger.
Deadlier than anything the world used to break me.**

One day, I will become someone they cannot drag again.
Someone they cannot humiliate again.
Someone they cannot silence again.

That day, the world bared its fangs.

But I lived long enough
to grow mine.

CHAPTER FIVE:

WHEN REBELLION BECAME A REFUGE

Before the BPO industry, I thought I knew myself.

I thought I was kind.
Disciplined.
Soft.
Responsible.
The good child.
The achiever.
The teacher who gave everything even when I had nothing.

But the BPO floor changed me.

It didn't just change me —
it cracked me open.

I entered the call center with one intention:

"Basin diri makabawi ko sa life."

And for a moment, it felt like that.

Suddenly, I was earning more than a teacher.
Suddenly, I could buy the things I once only stared at inside malls.
Suddenly, I wasn't starving...
I was spending.

But money without healing
is just another weapon you use against yourself.

And I was wounded in ways I refused to admit.

Becoming Maria Kim

The night shift introduced me to two names
that would mark an era of my life:

Jhay and Enzo.

They were fun.
Chaotic.
Brave.
Broken in the same places I was.
And without meaning to,
they opened the door to my own downfall.

One cigarette break turned into becoming a smoker.
One after-shift drink turned into early-morning intoxication.
One wild night turned into a habit.
One rebellion turned into a personality.

I wasn't abused anymore —
I was becoming the person the abuse created.

I was fiercer.
Sharper.
Louder.

I stopped apologizing.
I stopped shrinking.
I stopped letting people step on me.

When someone tried to bully me on the floor,
I spat fire back.
When people whispered about me,
I gave them something louder to talk about.

This was the era I learned how to bite back.

But it came with a price.

Becoming Maria Kim

My supervisor once called me into a room.
She said:

"You need to be more diligent."

I smiled.
Stood up.
Walked out.

And slacked off even harder.

When my Paid Time Off was denied,
I didn't negotiate.
I didn't beg.

I resigned.

Just like that.

Because for the first time in my life,
I wasn't afraid to walk away.

But freedom without direction?
It destroys you quietly.

I hopped from one company to another.
Looking for money, fun, validation —
anything that felt better than the pain I carried.

I didn't know it then,
but I was grieving my past self by trying to kill her.

I became maldita.
Confrontational.
Addicted to looking strong even when I was falling apart.

And worst of all —
I became a social climber.

I bragged everything on social media:

New phone.
New bag.
New shoes.
New purchases that meant nothing but felt like trophies.

Because deep inside,
I still felt poor.
Small.
Overlooked.

And I thought if people saw me shining —
even fakely —
maybe the world wouldn't see the wounds underneath.

But fake shine burns fast.

My spending became reckless.
My savings disappeared.
My habits controlled me.
And my family...
my responsibility to them became a burden I did not want to face.

I started giving less.
And I was ashamed of that.
But I didn't know how to choose them
when I was still learning how to choose myself.

I dated men
I knew didn't love me.
Men who only wanted money.
Men who saw me as convenience.
But I entertained them anyway.

Why?
Because broken people sometimes look for love in places that
confirm the same pain they already know.

It was not love.
It was loneliness dressed as romance.

Becoming Maria Kim

In the middle of this chaos,
I tried climbing the corporate ladder.

I attended training.
Tried applying for promotions.
Tried convincing myself that this was the path.

But every time the opportunity came close,
something in me pulled back.

I didn't belong there.
Not because I wasn't capable —
but because it didn't fulfill me.

There was no joy.
No purpose.
No meaning.

Just performance.
Pretending.
And pressure.

For so long, I lived for other people —
my parents, my siblings, my former students, society —
always trying to be good, responsible, respectable.

So when I finally had money and freedom,
I wanted to taste everything I was never allowed to taste.

Good or bad.
Light or dark.
Healthy or destructive.

And I did.

I tasted rebellion,
and rebellion tasted like survival.

Becoming Maria Kim

It was messy.
It was ugly.
It was dangerous.
But it felt like freedom.

The freedom to be flawed.
To be loud.
To be reckless.
To be someone who wasn't always the victim.

But freedom without healing
slowly turns you into someone you don't recognize.

One morning, after a long shift,
cigarette in hand,
alcohol in my breath,
eyes tired and empty,
I looked at myself in the mirror.

I didn't see the achiever anymore.
Or the teacher.
Or the dreamer.
Or the child who survived storms.

I saw a stranger.
A version of me shaped not by who I wanted to be
but by everything I was running from.

And that's when I realized:

I wasn't becoming bad.
I was becoming unhealed.

I was becoming the result
of every heartbreak,
every humiliation,
every injustice,
every moment the world showed its teeth.

Becoming Maria Kim

I wasn't evil.
I was wounded.
And I was acting like someone who didn't believe she deserved better.

It took me years to understand this truth:

Some people heal by breaking first.
Some people find themselves by getting lost.
Some people learn who they are
by becoming everything they swore they'd never become.

And that was me.

This was the era
where rebellion became my refuge.
Where chaos became my comfort.
Where destruction became my disguise.

But even then...
even at my worst...
somewhere deep inside me—
a part of me whispered:

"This is not your final form.
This is just the part where you burn
so you can rise."

CHAPTER SIX:

THE BATTLEFIELD WITHIN THE CLASSROOM

Getting into the public school system felt like redemption.

After years of stumbling through toxic workplaces and heartbreaks,
ranking **Top 5** in the DepEd hiring process felt like proof that the
achiever in me was still alive—
that no matter how much the world tried to break me,
I could still rise.

I was proud.
I was hopeful.
And for a moment... I was excited.

A new environment.
A respected institution.
Back to my profession,
back to the field where I once dreamed of making a difference.

But excitement fades fast
when the place you enter is built like a jungle.

Tejero Elementary School had its own ecosystem.

Its own politics.
Its own alliances.
Its own silent wars.

I didn't know it at first,
but I walked into a place where **seniority was power**,
and newcomers were often prey.

Mam Emma—kind, warm, and genuinely supportive—spoke highly
of me.
"Achiever na siya," she told them proudly.

She meant well.
But that praise became gasoline.

Whispers spread through the faculty room like wildfire.

"Bag-o pa lang pero hambogero daw."
"Achiever kuno. Pa-impress."
"Competition ni."

Some teachers welcomed me politely,
but most looked at me with thin smiles
and eyes that said:

"We're watching you."

I entered with a good reputation—
unfortunately, in environments like this,
a good reputation can feel like a threat.

My first real conflict came from a teacher I barely knew.

He used to be in charge of the Boy Scout office—
the same office I was newly assigned to manage.

When I first entered the room he left behind,
I almost gagged.

The place was a disaster.

Trash in corners.
Papers yellowed and molding.
Old trophies cracked and rusting.
A smell that clung to your clothes.

So I did what any responsible teacher would do:
I cleaned it.
I threw out the garbage.
I sanitized the chaos he abandoned.

Becoming Maria Kim

I didn't know
that by cleaning up his mess,
I was stepping into mine.

In the middle of my class—
in front of my students
and my co-teacher—
the door slammed open.

He walked in trembling with rage.

"Nganong imong gilabay akong mga butang?!"

My students froze.
My heart pounded.
I felt the room shrink.

Before I could respond, he shouted even louder.

"Wala kay respeto! Imong gi labay tanan! Kinsa man ka?"

I could feel my face flush with humiliation.
Not because he scolded me—
but because he did it publicly,
in front of children,
in front of colleagues,
in front of the entire world I was trying to belong to.

He stepped closer.
Closer.
Too close.

Then he jabbed his finger into my forehead.

Hard.
Twice.
Three times.

Becoming Maria Kim

A physical attack disguised as "discipline."

My co-teacher looked down—
silent, stiff, unmoving.

The silence was louder than his shouting.

It said:

"You're on your own."

When he left,
my class remained quiet, confused.
I swallowed everything—
my anger,
my tears,
my humiliation—
and finished the lesson with a voice that trembled through the pain.

By the time I stepped into the faculty room, the whole school knew.

Students whispered.
Teachers stared.
Some pretended to be concerned.
Others watched me like entertainment.

Public school is a jungle.

And in a jungle,
a wounded teacher is not protected—
they're circled.

That day, I learned:

**In DepEd, dogs eat dogs.
Respect isn't given—
it's fought for.
And sometimes survival requires claws.**

And in my heart, I whispered:

**"If they want a war,
they're going to meet the version of me
I spent years trying to bury."**

But the universe is balanced—
even in toxic spaces.

I met **Mylene and Richell**.

Two women so different from me,
they felt like the calm I never knew I needed.

Mylene was soft-spoken,
the type who reminded me to breathe before reacting.

Richell was grounded,
the type who reminded me that silence can be power too.

They didn't treat me like competition.
They didn't whisper about me.
They didn't judge.

They understood me.

Our friendship wasn't perfect—
we argued,
we misunderstood each other,
we had days where things felt off.

But they stayed.

In them, I found something rare:

People who don't abandon you in a place built to make you feel alone.

They taught me how to:

– soften without breaking
– stand my ground without losing myself
– choose battles wisely
– remain human in an inhumane environment
– stay humble even when others weren't

They reminded me:

**"Kim, dili ka kinahanglan musukol sa tanan.
Dili tanan away worth it."**

Sometimes, their calm felt like a life jacket.

Because if it weren't for them,
I would've become the version of myself my enemies wanted—
angry, bitter, and permanently hardened.

Instead...
I became strategic.
Observant.
Resilient.

I learned how to navigate the politics.
I learned whom to trust.
I learned whom to avoid.
I learned how to survive without losing my soul.

Looking back,
Tejero Elementary didn't just test me.

It revealed me.

I walked in hopeful, naive, eager to help.
I walked out stronger, sharper, unshakeable.

I learned that not every workplace nurtures you.
Some are meant to transform you.

Becoming Maria Kim

Some are meant to protect you from future suffering
by showing you what you will NEVER tolerate again.

Tejero was loud, cruel, political, dramatic—
but it was also the place that taught me:

I am not the underdog.
I am not easy to break.
I am not someone who fades quietly.

I survived that environment
not because I was the strongest
but because I refused to be destroyed.

I entered that school afraid.

I left it unmovable.

CHAPTER SEVEN:

THE MAN WHO BROKE ME, THE DEBT THAT DROWNED ME, AND THE DAY I LOST MYSELF

When people talk about their biggest mistake,
they often refer to a wrong decision, a wrong job, a wrong person.

But my mistake wasn't just one choice.

It was a slow, quiet collapse—
a spiral of loans, loneliness, pride, and the wrong kind of love.

It was a version of myself
I didn't recognize...

until it was too late.

It began with **loans**.

DepEd has a system—
one that moves faster than common sense.

Submit today.
Approved tomorrow.
Re-loan the next week.
Repeat monthly.

At first it felt liberating.
Then it felt convenient.
And eventually... it felt like the only thing keeping me alive.

I didn't realize I was borrowing from my own future.
From my own downfall.

And because my spending habits were already unhealthy—
my social climbing, my desire to look "okay,"

my longing to feel successful—
the loans became an addiction.

So I made a decision that felt brave at the time:

"Mag-negosyo ko."

I poured everything into an internet café near my school.
All my loans.
All my remaining salary.
All my energy.

The business was good at first.
Steady income.
Regular customers.
Students printing assignments.
Workers playing Dota 2 after shift.

But then I fell in love with the game, too.

Dota became my escape.
My coping mechanism.
My refuge from the life I didn't want to face.

And that's where I met **Jason.**

Jason.

Gwapo.
Soft-spoken.
Addict sa Dota in a charming way.
The kind of guy nga dili dapat mu-atensyon nako—
but he did.

He wasn't from our area,
but his friends played at my café,
and eventually,
so did he.

At first, admiration lang.
He was talented.
Quiet.
Focused.
And without realizing it…

my heartbeat began to betray me every time he walked in.

He was kind to me.
Respectful.
Approachable.
He talked to me like a person,
not like a joke,
not like an easy target.

Slowly,
he turned my café into his tambayan…

…then into my comfort…

…and eventually into the place where my biggest heartbreak would
begin.

One day, Jason got sick.
I brought him food, medication, towels—
everything.

And that's where **we confessed to each other.**

He liked me.
I liked him.

Before long,
we became "us."

He moved in with me.
And with him came the expenses—

food, rent, electricity, clothes, allowance,
the things he needed,
and the things he just wanted.

But I gave.
And gave.
And gave.

Because when you finally feel "chosen,"
you don't notice you're being used.

I convinced myself it was love.
But what I didn't see was this:

I wasn't building a relationship.
I was funding it.

And as Jason's life got easier,
mine began to collapse.

My business was bleeding.
My debts doubled.
My salary? Gone before it arrived.

Still, I continued.

Because love, when mixed with emptiness,
becomes desperation.

Our relationship turned toxic.
We fought.
We screamed.
We broke up and reconciled.
Cycle after cycle.
Pain after pain.

I became jealous, paranoid, obsessive.

Becoming Maria Kim

I hacked his Facebook.
His messages.
His phone.

And there—
every suspicion confirmed.

He wasn't loyal.
Not even close.
He entertained others.

Not just girls.
Not just one person.
Many.

And yet…
I stayed.

Because sometimes,
you stay not because of love—
but because you've already lost everything else.

Money gone.
Business declining.
Savings destroyed.
Family disappointed.
Pride shattered.

Jason was the only thing I was holding onto.

Even if he was also the one drowning me.

We could no longer afford rent,
so we moved to a tiny space,
renting a corner in someone else's house.

We slept in the sala.
No privacy.

Becoming Maria Kim

No dignity.
No stability.

I thought he would stay because of love.

But he stayed because of comfort.
And when that comfort disappeared…
so did he.

One night, in the rain,
I begged him to stay.

The strongest parts of me—
the fighter, the achiever, the survivor—
all collapsed in front of him.

He looked at me,
cold, sure, unbothered—

and said:

"Di ko ganahan makigbalik nimo."

Then he walked away.

Leaving me standing there,
soaked, shaking,
broken in ways I couldn't explain.

My family wasn't speaking to me.
I hadn't contributed in months.
My father was furious.
My siblings disappointed.

My friends?
I abandoned them for Jason
so when he left,
I had no one.

Becoming Maria Kim

Not a single person to run to.
Not a single shoulder to cry on.
No home, no business, no money, no support.

Even my internet café—
my last source of income—
collapsed completely.

I had nothing left.

And when a person loses everything externally,
their inner world begins to crumble too.

That was when the darkest thought entered my mind:

"Siguro… mas maayo pa muundang nalang ko sa tanan."
"Wala naman koy ugma."
"Wala nakoy rason."

I stared at that thought
too long,
too closely,
too dangerously.

But this is not where my story ends.

Because sometimes,
you need to break
to learn your worth.

Sometimes,
you need to lose everything
to find yourself again.

This was the ugliest fall of my life…
but also the beginning
of the version of me
who would one day rise beyond every storm.

CHAPTER EIGHT:

THE NIGHT I ALMOST DISAPPEARED — AND THE GOD WHO SAW ME

Losing money is painful.
Losing love is heartbreaking.
But losing *everything*—
your home, your dignity, your purpose—
is a different kind of death.

And that's exactly where my life collapsed.

Not just broke.
Not just heartbroken.
Not just lost.

I became homeless.

No bed.
No room.
No comfort.
No family to run to.
No friends left to call.
No peso in my pocket for food.
No roof except the roof of the classroom where I taught.

My entire world crumbled so completely
that the only place left to hide
was the place where I used to stand the strongest:

inside my own classroom.

At night, when the last student went home
and the hallways turned silent,
I would slip back inside like a shadow.

Becoming Maria Kim

Close the lights.
Lock the door.
Lie on the cold floor.
Hug myself to sleep.

The same room where I taught children about hope
became the room where I silently tried to survive.

I tried not to cry,
but tears don't ask for permission.

I was starving.
I was exhausted.
I was ashamed.

I bought a small plastic container from a sidewalk vendor
because that was all I could afford.
And inside that dark classroom—
my temporary shelter—
I cooked instant noodles quietly, praying no one would hear or see me.

That was my dinner.
Sometimes my only meal.

Every night felt like a punishment—
a long echo of all the wrong choices I made,
the wrong love I fought for,
the wrong loans I signed,
the wrong things I chased.

But I couldn't undo anything.

I could only live with it.

I woke up before 4AM every day
to hide the evidence—

the blanket, the spare clothes, the small container.
I didn't want anyone to discover the truth.

But secrets eventually betray you.

Some students noticed.
Some teachers noticed.
My weight was dropping fast.
My uniform hung loosely.
My face was pale.
My eyes were empty.

Teacher Rowena became an unexpected angel.
No questions asked
—she would just leave food on my table.
A sandwich.
A packed meal.
Sometimes rice.

Because she knew.
She could feel it.

There were days
when even buying bread was impossible.

But even those moments
weren't the worst.

One morning, my principal called me to her office.
Her expression was stern.
Her voice was cold.

"I know you've been sleeping in your classroom.
You need to leave.
Find a place TODAY."

My world stopped.

Becoming Maria Kim

Where would I go?
How would I pay?
What could I possibly do?

I had nothing.
Absolutely nothing.

But fate still had a sliver of mercy.

A co-teacher—someone I barely talked to—
offered to lend me ₱2,000
so I could find a bedspace.

Her kindness was enough to make me cry.

That same day, a friend referred me to a nearby room.
₱1,500 a month.
Walking distance to school.

I gathered my few belongings,
and under the heavy rain,
I moved.

I slipped on broken glass on the road,
cutting my foot deeply.

Blood mixed with the rain.
Pain mixed with exhaustion.
Shame mixed with surrender.

Kung minamalas ka nga naman…
minsan sunod-sunod.
Walang pahinga.

The bedspace was tiny—
barely enough for me to turn.
But it was a door.
A roof.
A place to exist.

And that alone was a miracle.

But miracles sometimes appear after the darkest temptations.

That night,
still shaking from everything,
I wandered aimlessly.

I climbed to a rooftop of a building with an internet café—
a place overlooking the city lights.

It was raining hard.
The cold wind slapped my skin.
The world felt blurry.

And then...
a dangerous thought entered my mind:

"Kung muambak ko diri, matapos tanang sakit."

I stepped closer to the ledge.

My life flashed in fragments—
my childhood,
my family,
my dreams,
my failures.

I felt nothing.
Just emptiness.

But then—

through the rain,
across the open rooftop,
in the distance illuminated by dim lights—

I saw it.

**The image of Señor Sto. Niño
at the Basilica.**

Calm.
Steady.
Watching.

My knees weakened.
My soul cracked open.

I sobbed—
not quietly,
but the kind of sobbing that comes from the deepest wound in your
heart.

I talked to Sto. Niño through the rain:

"Tabangi ko.
Kapoy na kaayo ko.
Ayaw ko biya-i."

And in that moment,
I felt something lift from my chest—
a heaviness I carried for too long.

For the first time in months,
I felt...

hope.

A warmth.
A presence.
A divine intervention.

Sto. Niño didn't give me answers—
but He gave me strength to step away from the edge.

Becoming Maria Kim

I went back inside the internet café,
still trembling.

I opened Facebook,
just to distract my mind.

And then I saw her—
Stell—
my friend now teaching in the United States.

I messaged her.
Not to ask for money.
Not to ask for rescue.

I asked for a chance:

"Stell, tabangi ko apply sa US.
Maski unsa.
Maski asa."

She replied.

She said yes.
She gave me guidelines.
She encouraged me.

And then another friend—**Nellene**—reached out to help too.

Suddenly,
after months of drowning in darkness…

I had a direction.

I reworked my résumé that same night.
I started gathering requirements.
I fixed my documents.
I applied everywhere I could.

Becoming Maria Kim

Later that night,
I saw an opening for a part-time job.
I applied immediately.

There, in that small bedspace,
with my bandaged foot
and my tired eyes—

I felt something shift.

A spark.
A will.
A whisper of resilience.

"This is the beginning," I told myself.
"I am not dead yet."

Because sometimes,
the universe takes everything from you
not to punish you—
but to rebuild you
from the ashes.

And this was the night
I chose to rise again.

CHAPTER NINE:

THE NIGHT I ALMOST DISAPPEARED — AND THE GOD WHO SAW ME

Losing money is painful.
Losing love is heartbreaking.
But losing *everything*—
your home, your dignity, your purpose—
is a different kind of death.

And that's exactly where my life collapsed.

Not just broke.
Not just heartbroken.
Not just lost.

I became homeless.

No bed.
No room.
No comfort.
No family to run to.
No friends left to call.
No peso in my pocket for food.
No roof except the roof of the classroom where I taught.

My entire world crumbled so completely
that the only place left to hide
was the place where I used to stand the strongest:

inside my own classroom.

At night, when the last student went home
and the hallways turned silent,
I would slip back inside like a shadow.

Becoming Maria Kim

Close the lights.
Lock the door.
Lie on the cold floor.
Hug myself to sleep.

The same room where I taught children about hope
became the room where I silently tried to survive.

I tried not to cry,
but tears don't ask for permission.

I was starving.
I was exhausted.
I was ashamed.

I bought a small plastic container from a sidewalk vendor
because that was all I could afford.
And inside that dark classroom—
my temporary shelter—
**I cooked instant noodles quietly, praying no one would hear or
see me.**

That was my dinner.
Sometimes my only meal.

Every night felt like a punishment—
a long echo of all the wrong choices I made,
the wrong love I fought for,
the wrong loans I signed,
the wrong things I chased.

But I couldn't undo anything.

I could only live with it.

I woke up before 4AM every day
to hide the evidence—

the blanket, the spare clothes, the small container.
I didn't want anyone to discover the truth.

But secrets eventually betray you.

Some students noticed.
Some teachers noticed.
My weight was dropping fast.
My uniform hung loosely.
My face was pale.
My eyes were empty.

Teacher Rowena became an unexpected angel.
No questions asked
—she would just leave food on my table.
A sandwich.
A packed meal.
Sometimes rice.

Because she knew.
She could feel it.

There were days
when even buying bread was impossible.

But even those moments
weren't the worst.

One morning, my principal called me to her office.
Her expression was stern.
Her voice was cold.

"I know you've been sleeping in your classroom.
You need to leave.
Find a place TODAY."

My world stopped.

Becoming Maria Kim

Where would I go?
How would I pay?
What could I possibly do?

I had nothing.
Absolutely nothing.

But fate still had a sliver of mercy.

A co-teacher—someone I barely talked to—
offered to lend me ₱2,000
so I could find a bedspace.

Her kindness was enough to make me cry.

That same day, a friend referred me to a nearby room.
₱1,500 a month.
Walking distance to school.

I gathered my few belongings,
and under the heavy rain,
I moved.

I slipped on broken glass on the road,
cutting my foot deeply.

Blood mixed with the rain.
Pain mixed with exhaustion.
Shame mixed with surrender.

Kung minamalas ka nga naman...
minsan sunod-sunod.
Walang pahinga.

The bedspace was tiny—
barely enough for me to turn.
But it was a door.
A roof.
A place to exist.

And that alone was a miracle.

But miracles sometimes appear after the darkest temptations.

That night,
still shaking from everything,
I wandered aimlessly.

I climbed to a rooftop of a building with an internet café—
a place overlooking the city lights.

It was raining hard.
The cold wind slapped my skin.
The world felt blurry.

And then...
a dangerous thought entered my mind:

"Kung muambak ko diri, matapos tanang sakit."

I stepped closer to the ledge.

My life flashed in fragments—
my childhood,
my family,
my dreams,
my failures.

I felt nothing.
Just emptiness.

But then—

through the rain,
across the open rooftop,
in the distance illuminated by dim lights—

I saw it.

**The image of Señor Sto. Niño
at the Basilica.**

Calm.
Steady.
Watching.

My knees weakened.
My soul cracked open.

I sobbed—
not quietly,
but the kind of sobbing that comes from the deepest wound in your
heart.

I talked to Sto. Niño through the rain:

"Tabangi ko.
Kapoy na kaayo ko.
Ayaw ko biya-i."

And in that moment,
I felt something lift from my chest—
a heaviness I carried for too long.

For the first time in months,
I felt...

hope.

A warmth.
A presence.
A divine intervention.

Sto. Niño didn't give me answers—
but He gave me strength to step away from the edge.

Becoming Maria Kim

I went back inside the internet café,
still trembling.

I opened Facebook,
just to distract my mind.

And then I saw her—
Stell—
my friend now teaching in the United States.

I messaged her.
Not to ask for money.
Not to ask for rescue.

I asked for a chance:

"Stell, tabangi ko apply sa US.
Maski unsa.
Maski asa."

She replied.

She said yes.
She gave me guidelines.
She encouraged me.

And then another friend—**Nellene**—reached out to help too.

Suddenly,
after months of drowning in darkness...

I had a direction.

I reworked my résumé that same night.
I started gathering requirements.
I fixed my documents.
I applied everywhere I could.

Becoming Maria Kim

Later that night,
I saw an opening for a part-time job.
I applied immediately.

There, in that small bedspace,
with my bandaged foot
and my tired eyes—

I felt something shift.

A spark.
A will.
A whisper of resilience.

"This is the beginning," I told myself.
"I am not dead yet."

Because sometimes,
the universe takes everything from you
not to punish you—
but to rebuild you
from the ashes.

And this was the night
I chose to rise again.

CHAPTER TEN:

WHEN GOD OPENED DOORS — AND MY HEART OPENED THE WRONG ONE

When you survive your darkest night,
you don't expect blessings to arrive one after another.
You expect more storms.
More pain.
More consequences chasing you.

But life surprised me.

Because when I chose to rise,
the universe finally chose to lift me.

I applied for a part-time job as a Customer Service Associate in a BPO company —
just something small, something to help me get by.

But during the interview,
the manager looked at my résumé,
listened to how I spoke,
watched how I carried myself...

and hired me not as a part-timer,
not as a CSR,
but as a **full-time Social Media Manager.**

For the first time in a long time,
I felt something I thought I had lost:

Pride.
Competence.
Self-worth.

Becoming Maria Kim

It felt like God was whispering,
"Wala ka nawala.
Gipuyan lang nimo imong kasakit."

My boss, Jeff, saw potential in me.
He saw talent beneath my exhaustion.
He saw capability beneath my wounds.

He allowed me to work two full-time jobs.

Yes —
I was a teacher by day
and a social media manager by night.

I impressed him.
Every output I submitted was polished, precise, creative —
even when I was doing it during short breaks
or in the quiet moments of my classroom.

I barely slept.

I slept from 5 PM to 10 PM,
woke up, worked,
then went to the office by 11 PM.

My body was tired,
but my soul was alive.

And because I gave everything I had,
my performance soared so high
my salary was increased to **₱50,000**.

It was the first time I felt financially secure.
The first time I could breathe.
The first time I tasted freedom.

But I didn't stop there.

Becoming Maria Kim

I worked harder.
Smarter.
Better.

Soon, I was promoted to **Operations Manager**,
earning **₱200,000** a month.

From sleeping on classroom floors
to earning more than I ever imagined—

I cried.

Because this time,
the tears weren't from pain.

They were from redemption.

I used my blessings wisely.
I fixed the things I broke.

I reached out to my mother,
secretly sending her money.
I wasn't ready to face my father yet —
and maybe he wasn't ready to face me either.

I reconnected with friends,
and they celebrated my comeback
because they remembered the woman who nearly disappeared.

I learned financial discipline.
I controlled my spending.
I made smarter choices.
I matured.

I even afforded my own condo.
I bought what I needed
without guilt,

without fear,
without shame.

For the first time in years,
life finally felt steady.
Peaceful.
Bright.

**Finally, I felt like I wasn't just surviving...
I was winning.**

Everything was perfect.

Until it wasn't.

One day, Jeff told me:

"Hire an assistant. Someone who can help you handle your workload."

And just like that,
a single instruction
awakened something in me
I didn't want to acknowledge.

My mind scanned possibilities—
but my heart whispered a name
I thought I had buried:

Jason.

Yes — him.
The man who shattered me.
The man who left me in the rain.
The man who drained my money, my peace, my dignity.
The man who broke me so deeply
I almost ended my life.

And yet...
my heart betrayed me.

I told myself it was "to help him,"
so he could work
and not depend on others.

But deep inside,
I knew the truth.

Mahal ko pa rin siya.

So I reached out.
Through one of his friends.
I spread the word about the job opening.

I interviewed several applicants fairly.
Professionally.

But I knew who I was waiting for.

And then he arrived.

The last applicant of the day.

When he walked into the room,
my chest tightened.
My palms sweated.
My throat dried.

Dapat siya ang kaba-kabaon.
Dapat siya ang murag mu-ubo sa tensyon.
Dapat siya ang uneasy in front of me.

But no.

Ako.

Ako ang na-panic.
Ako ang nanotice sa akong heartbeat.
Ako ang na-paralyze sa presence niya.

He sat across from me,
and for a moment I pretended to be busy
just to collect myself.

But eventually,
I forced myself to look at him.

And just like that—

everything I worked so hard to bury,
everything I tried to forget,
every memory I survived...

came rushing back.

Shit.
I am still in love with him.

And that truth hurt more
than every night I slept on a cold classroom floor.

More
than hunger.
More
than debt.
More
than humiliation.
More
than losing everything.

Because I realized:

Success can rebuild your life...
but it cannot erase your wounds.

Becoming Maria Kim

You can fix your finances.
You can rise in your career.
You can restore relationships.
You can heal your pride.

But the heart heals last.

The heart remembers what the mind wants to forget.
The heart recognizes the face
that once destroyed it.
The heart breaks quietly
even at the peak of your success.

And in that small office,
with Jason sitting across from me
like a ghost I invited back into my new life,

I understood another painful truth:

**Even the strongest comeback
can crumble with one familiar face.**

And yet...
despite everything...

**I still wanted to help him.
I still cared.
I still loved him.**

I hated myself for it.

But I couldn't deny it.

Not to him.
Not to myself.
Not to God.

And as he waited for my decision,
as he looked at me with those eyes I once surrendered everything
to...

I felt the ground shifting again.

**Because the next part of my story
would begin with one choice:**

Will I hire him?

(To be continued...)

CHAPTER ELEVEN:

THE MOMENT MY HEART BET AGAINST MY MIND

I hired him.

It felt wrong.
It felt foolish.
It felt like stepping back into a fire I once barely escaped.

But my heart...
my fragile, stubborn, traitorous heart...

was happy.

Happy in a way that frightened me.
Happy in a way that felt like betrayal to the woman I had become.
Happy in a way that only old love—
the kind that almost destroyed you—
can resurrect.

I started looking forward to work.
To mornings.
To brief glances.
To hallway encounters.
To the quiet joy of knowing he was just a few desks away.

I was his boss now.
Imagine the irony.

And I didn't even understand what went through my mind the day I
hired him.
Maybe I thought:

"This time, I can finally be enough.
This time, I have stability.
This time, I won't be the broken one."

Maybe I thought fate was giving us one last try.
Maybe I thought love was circling back.
Maybe I thought money could finally make me worthy.

But I also didn't want to lie to myself anymore.

So I whispered the only shield I ever had
against decisions I wasn't proud of:

"Bahala na."

Ordinary days at work suddenly became small, dangerous moments.

Moments that made my heart skip.
Moments that made my chest feel tight.
Moments that made my mind roll its eyes at my heart.

Yes—
nagpakatanga na sad ko.

At first, I convinced myself the feeling would fade.
I told myself:

**"Colleague ra na siya.
You're older now.
You're wiser now.
You're healed now."**

But I wasn't.

Every day I noticed myself slowly falling again.
Gently at first.
Then carelessly.
Then completely.

We ate meals together.
Sometimes he brought me food.
Sometimes we went home at the same time.

Becoming Maria Kim

Sometimes we drank with coworkers
and my eyes were always—
always—
on him.

I tried to be mature.
Professional.
Cold.
Detached.

But the heart never listens to logic.

And many nights during inuman,
I found myself fighting the urge to kiss him—
not out of lust,
but out of longing so old and so deep
it felt like a part of my identity.

But I controlled myself.
I was terrified of being rejected again.
Terrified of becoming the girl who begged in the rain.

I didn't want to relive that version of me.

Then came the team building in **Camotes Island**.

Our second time there.
The first was when we were lovers.
This time, we were coworkers...
or so I tried to convince myself.

But the truth?

I chose Camotes on purpose.

A part of me believed
that maybe if we returned to the same island—
the same sea,

the same horizon,
the same memories—

maybe we would return to each other too.

It was foolish.
It was hopeful.
It was human.

The night was beautiful—
the sky full of stars,
the air warm,
the ocean soft and rhythmic.

Everyone was drunk and laughing,
except us.

Jason and I found ourselves alone by the beach,
listening to the waves crash gently against the shore.

It felt almost cinematic.
Almost fated.

Then he spoke.

"I'm sorry sa tanan.
Sa gibuhat nako sauna.
Sa wala nako pagtuo nimo."

His voice cracked.
His eyes softened
in a way I had never seen when we were still together.

He told me he was proud of me—
proud of what I had become,
proud of how far I had come.

My chest tightened.

For a moment,
the entire world paused.

**"Is this it?
Is this our moment?"**

I couldn't breathe.
My heart was pounding so wildly
I thought I would faint.

I told him:

"This success…
wouldn't have happened if you didn't leave.
You were my inspiration.
I wanted to prove to you
that I could make life happen again."

He looked down,
embarrassed,
ashamed,
quiet.

The silence felt like a fragile bridge
waiting for someone to take the first step.

I swallowed hard
and gathered courage from a place in me
I didn't know still existed.

I asked him:

"Did you really love me?"

He answered yes.

And even though I knew deep inside it wasn't fully true,
my foolish heart still believed him.
Still fluttered.
Still felt fifteen all over again.

But I wasn't done.

There was one more question—
the question that could save me
or destroy me all over again.

My voice trembled.

"How about now?
Do you still have any feelings left for me?
May kakarampot pa ba na pag-ibig dyan...
para sa akin?
Kasi ako...
hanggang ngayon...
ikaw pa rin."

He looked at me.

His eyes were red.
Teary.
Unsteady.
Conflicted.

He stared at me like he was holding back something heavy,
dangerous,
honest,
real.

He opened his lips...

...and right before the words came out—

the night, the stars, the waves, and my heartbeat all froze.

Because whatever he was about to say
would change everything.

[To be continued...]

CHAPTER TWELVE:

THE ANSWER THAT BROKE ME—AGAIN

The moment I finished my question,
the world around me shifted.

I felt dizzy.
Like the stars were spinning.
Like the sand beneath me was moving.
Like the entire island suddenly tilted.

My stomach tightened—
not butterflies,
but something sharp…
like a punch from the inside.

My heart pounded so fast
I thought I was going to faint.

Then he took a breath.

A long, heavy, devastating breath.

And said the words that shattered me:

"I'm sorry… pero I see you as a friend."

Just a friend.
Those three words hit harder than any heartbreak I ever had.

He continued:

**"I respect you as my boss.
I don't want mobalik nasad ang atong past kay nindut nata'g
relasyon karon."**

He talked about *respect*.
He talked about *our good relationship now*.

Becoming Maria Kim

He talked about the *past* like it was a stain
we should be careful not to spill again.

But all I heard was:

"There is no us.
Not now.
Not anymore."

I wanted the earth to swallow me whole.
Right there.
Right on that beach.
Right under that starry sky
that had fooled me into believing
I had one more chance.

My face burned.
My ears rang.
My chest tightened.

I felt humiliated.
Embarrassed.
Stupid.
Small.

"Shit," I whispered to myself.
"Another rejection."

My eyes filled with tears before I could stop them.
I wanted to disappear.
I wanted to vanish into the waves,
into the darkness,
into anything that wasn't this moment.

But all I managed to say was:

"I understand."

Becoming Maria Kim

Did I really?
Or was I just lying to survive the moment?

Was I understanding him…
or was I hoping he would change his mind?

I apologized for making the conversation awkward,
trying to regain dignity I didn't even have left.

He shook his head gently.

**"No… it's okay.
Mas maayo nga naistoryahan nato ni
para dili ka naga-asa."**

Para *hindi na ako umasa.*

Those words cut deeper
because hope was the only thing that kept me breathing
for days, weeks, months.

I forced myself to stand.

"Tulog sa ko," I lied.

But instead of going back to my room,
I walked silently to the far end of the beach
where the moon touched the water
and the whole world felt painfully quiet.

And there—
far from him,
far from the laughter of others,
far from the memories I tried to revive—

I broke.

I cried like a child.
I cried like a heart that had been promised a miracle
only to receive another wound.

Becoming Maria Kim

I cried like someone who was tired—
tired of trying,
tired of loving,
tired of hoping for someone
who never hoped for me.

Was I crying because of him?

Or was I crying
because for the millionth time,
I felt unchosen?

Unwanted?
Unworthy?

I asked myself over and over:

**"Will someone like me ever be loved?
What do I need to do?
Am I not enough?
What is wrong with me?"**

The waves didn't answer.
The sky didn't answer.
My heart didn't answer.

I went back to my room
with swollen eyes
and a silence so loud it hurt.

I lay in bed, shivering, exhausted,
my mind drowning in questions
that had no answers.

But one truth echoed in my chest
before I fell asleep:

**I was tired of being the one
who loved too much
and was loved too little.**

And for the first time that night,
I admitted the thought I feared the most:

Maybe I was not made to be loved.

(To be continued...)

CHAPTER THIRTEEN:

THE BEGINNING OF THE MAN I WAS MEANT TO BECOME

The day after Camotes felt heavier than the heartbreak itself.

I saw him approaching…
but I couldn't look at him.

He sat beside me like nothing happened,
like the night before was just another memory
meant to dissolve into the ocean.

But I couldn't breathe next to him.

I pretended someone was calling,
stood up,
and moved to another seat.

It was the most cowardly way to avoid a person—
yet the bravest way I knew how to protect what was left of me.

I wasn't avoiding him only because he rejected me.
I was avoiding him
because I was scared
that if I stayed close…

I would hope again.
I would fall again.
I would lose myself again.

And God knows
I could not afford to die twice from the same love.

Back at the office,
it was torture.

I made him my secretary—
my biggest mistake.
His desk was only a few meters away.
Every time he typed,
every time he looked up,
every time he said "Sir"...
my chest tightened.

I forced myself to become cold.
Short replies.
Neutral tone.
Avoiding his eyes.

But he noticed.

He texted.

"Are you okay?"
"Pwede ta mag inum?"
"Talk ta bi."

God, how I wanted to say yes.
But I forced myself to say no.
Every. Single. Time.

This time,
I promised myself:

"I will choose me."

But deep inside,
I kept asking one impossible question:

"How do I get rid of Jason when he is standing right in front of me?"

And then it happened.

Becoming Maria Kim

The moment that proved
God listens even to the whispers we say only to ourselves.

I received an email.

Foreign name.
Foreign school.
Foreign opportunity.

I stared at it for a full minute
before my brain caught up with reality:

**A school abroad wanted to interview me.
Not just any school—
a school in the United States.**

I almost forgot that my friends, Stell and Nellene,
submitted applications for me months ago.

Suddenly my chest felt strange.
Not the pain I felt with Jason—
but something else.

Fear?
Excitement?
Uncertainty?
Hope?

I didn't know.

What if I passed?
What if this was my one chance
to rewrite my entire life?

But then I looked around me—
my office,
my salary,
my position,
my comfort.

Becoming Maria Kim

Was I really happy?

Or was I just comfortable
because I had money
and Jason was nearby?

I decided to say yes to the interview.

The school loved me.
Then another school emailed.
Then another.

Three interviews.
Three job offers.
Three doors opening
all at the same time.

My heart stopped.
My mind raced.

I was being asked to choose my future.

When I told my boss—an American—
that I was considering a teaching job in the US,
he panicked.

He increased my salary
to match the teacher's pay in America.
₱250,000 per month.

It was insane.
Unreal.
Life-changing.

I said yes to him.

But this time...
I was smarter.

I continued my US application in secret.

Because something inside me whispered:

**"This is your only chance.
Don't waste it for comfort.
Don't waste it for a man.
Don't waste it for fear."**

I went to Manila for my embassy interview.

I failed.

I cried that night.

Maybe this wasn't for me.
Maybe I was meant to stay.
Maybe my life was supposed to begin and end in Cebu.

But then I told myself:

**"One more try.
If it still fails... maybe America isn't mine."**

I returned for my second interview.

The officer smiled.
Asked deeper questions.
Looked impressed.
And before I knew it—

"Your visa is approved."

My passport was taken for printing.

And suddenly...
everything went silent.

I was leaving.
The Philippines.
My home.

Becoming Maria Kim

My comfort.
My pain.
My past.
Jason.

I wasn't ready.
I wasn't sure.
I wasn't even fully grasping what was happening.

But a small voice inside me whispered:

"Maybe you'll find love in the US."

I told no one.
Not my coworkers.
Not even Jason.
Not until my flight was near.

I talked to my father for the first time in years.
Face to face.
Heart to heart.

"I want to make you proud,"
I told him
as tears spilled from my eyes.

My mother held me,
crying silently.
My brother was emotional.
My father...
the man who once beat me for being gay...
looked at me with something I had longed for all my life—
fear of losing me.
Love.
Worry.
Pride.

We didn't have much time.
A week passed quickly.

Then the day came.

The airport.
The goodbye.
The moment that hurt more than any breakup.

Seeing my parents behind the glass,
waving,
smiling through tears,
praying for me,
hoping for me,
loving me—

It broke me deeper than Jason ever did.

Because this time,
the goodbye wasn't rejection.
It wasn't betrayal.
It wasn't unrequited love.

It was love letting me go
so I could finally grow.

When I stepped into the airplane,
I felt my old life fall away—
every heartbreak,
every humiliation,
every insult,
every rejection,
every scar.

I whispered to myself:

"WELCOME TO THE NEW YOU, KENNETH."

And for the first time in a very long time—
I felt ready.

(To be continued...)

CHAPTER FOURTEEN:

WELCOME TO AMERICA — THE LAND WHERE I MET THE NEW ME

The moment I stepped foot in the United States,
something inside me cracked wide open.

Excitement.
Freedom.
Relief.
A childlike wonder I hadn't felt in years.

For a brief, sparkling moment,
I forgot every pain, every heartbreak, every rejection I carried from home.

I was like a kid entering Toy Kingdom for the first time.

LAX looked magical.
Bright lights.
Huge terminals.
Everything sparkling with the illusion of the "American Dream."

I remember thinking:

**"This is it.
This is the life I prayed for."**

Funny…
because now,
I hate that airport.
Chaotic. Crowded.
Pero at that moment?
It was heaven.

Becoming Maria Kim

The journey to my final destination felt long.
Los Angeles to Albuquerque, New Mexico.
A world away from Cebu.
A world away from everything familiar.

When I arrived,
everything was dark—
the sky, the city, even my mood.

Nothing looked like the America I imagined.
No skyscrapers.
No Times Square lights.
No Hollywood glow.

Just quiet streets,
frozen air,
and a coldness that felt like it could swallow you whole.

Winter welcomed me
like an icy hand gripping my chest.

As I inhaled the freezing air,
the cold reminded me of everything I left behind—
my mother's hugs,
my father's complicated love,
my brother's presence,
my friends' laughter.

And the pain I thought I buried on the plane
found its way back into my throat.

But I kept moving.

Inside the hotel room,
surrounded by suitcases and silence,
I unpacked my things with trembling hands.

Becoming Maria Kim

My life—
my entire life—
fit inside 2 balikbayan boxes.

But somehow,
the room felt full of possibility.

I took a picture at LAX earlier,
the American flag behind me,
"Welcome to Los Angeles" glowing in the background,
and I posted it on Facebook.

Within minutes—
my phone exploded.

Messages.
Comments.
Missed calls.

Some were shocked.
Some were happy.
Some were hurt I didn't tell them.
Some couldn't believe it.

But for the first time,
in a very long time…

I felt seen.

And this time,
not because of heartbreak,
not because of failure,
not because of drama—

But because I made it.

This was the beginning.

Alone in a foreign country,
my loneliness did what any single gay person would do:

I downloaded a dating app.

Swipe here.
Swipe there.
Swipe left — "Ew, no."
Swipe right — "Pwede."

I wasn't even looking for love.
I was just… curious.
Alive.
Free.
And still riding the high of my American arrival.

The next day,
reality hit.

All my friends were at work.
No one could guide me.
No one could pick me up.
No one could tour me around.

So I did everything myself.

Documents.
School paperwork.
Agency requirements.
Exploring a foreign city alone.

It was scary.
But also adventurous.

I told myself:

**"Kung nakatulog ko sa classroom for months,
ito pa kaya?"**

But the weather was brutal.

Dry skin.
Dry throat.
Dry lips.
Dry everything.

I couldn't breathe properly.
I thought:

"Ginoo ko, mamatay ba ko diri?"

Turns out...
water lang pala.
My dramatic ass was overreacting.

But I survived.
I was enjoying.
I felt proud.
I was earning dollars.

Life finally felt good again.

And then the momentum shifted.

My agency called.

No available room for me.
No housing options.
No host family.
Only one choice:

Live in the dining room of a stranger's house.

I didn't even blink.

"Sige. I'll take it."

Becoming Maria Kim

They covered the dining area with a curtain
to create a "room."
A curtain.
As in literal kurtina lang.
Not even thick enough to block the smell of cooking.

Every morning,
my roommates cooked breakfast
and the aroma—
fried eggs, oil, onions—
would weave its way into my clothes.

I slept beside the kitchen table.
I stored my things in a tiny cabinet.
I had a single bed,
barely enough for my body.

But there was a heater.
A roof.
Privacy.
Warmth.

And I told myself:

**"This is still better than what I had before.
I won't complain.
I'm earning dollars now."**

That tiny space…
that cramped, curtain-covered dining room…

felt like a blessing.

Because even though it wasn't ideal,
it wasn't the classroom floor.
It wasn't homelessness.
It wasn't rejection.
It wasn't despair.

Becoming Maria Kim

It was the beginning of my dream.

It was my stepping stone.

It was my survival.

And from that little corner of someone else's house,
sleeping beside pots and pans,
I whispered to myself:

"I am here.
I am alive.
I am starting again."

And for the first time…
America didn't feel like a place.
It felt like a second chance.

(To be continued…)

CHAPTER FIFTEEN:

THE HELLO THAT CHANGED EVERYTHING

Starting my new life as a teacher in America felt surreal.

The first time I stepped inside my classroom—
in a real U.S. school, with real U.S. students,
and real U.S. expectations—
my heart whispered:

"You made it, Kenneth."

But there was also fear.
Culture shock.
Pressure.

American students were different.
Independent.
Direct.
Sometimes overly frank.

And the system?
Ay, lahi ra jud.
The paperwork.
The expectations.
The standards.

Pero laban.

Kenneth always rises when challenged.

I worked hard.
I adapted.
I learned fast.
I taught even faster.

Becoming Maria Kim

But somewhere between lesson plans, trainings,
and navigating American culture...
something felt missing.

Something na dugay na nakong gi-crave.

Something na wala pa'y sign sa akong life:

Romance.

One night, I remembered the dating app I downloaded.
Out of boredom, curiosity, and a bit of loneliness.

When I checked it,
I saw a few messages—
some sweet,
some weird,
most of them...
nasty.
NSFW surprise videos.
Old men.
Married men.
Hook-up culture everywhere.

Dating in America was a different battlefield.

And me?
Wala kaayo'y nagtan-aw.
Walay Troy Bolton nga mo-swoop in.

Who would've thought?
The girl at LAX with an American flag behind him—
was not a popular choice here.

Men here are not impressed by money.
Wala silay pake kung manager ka sa Pilipinas.
They want muscles.

Becoming Maria Kim

They want masculine.
They want tall.

And I was...
none of those.

I went on a few dates,
pero walay spark.
Walay kilig.
Walay chemistry.

Truth is—
I was too picky for someone
who didn't even stand out in the American market.

Three months passed,
and finally
I moved to a real apartment.

A real room.
A bigger space.
Privacy.
Warmth.

And fate stepped in through a person named **Will**.

He was a makeup artist-slash-teacher.
Creative.
Confident.
Colorful.
Exactly the kind of person fate sends
when it wants you to discover something new about yourself.

"You would look so pretty with makeup,"
Will said casually.

I laughed.
Hard.
"Girl, please. Have you seen me?"
I said.

But Will insisted.

He said my bone structure, my small frame, my face—
ALL had potential.
Ako daw mismo ang nag-limit sa akong beauty
because of fear, judgment, and the Philippines' harsh culture.

One day, bored and lonely,
I finally said:

"Sige na, transform me."

We shopped for makeup,
lashes,
foundation,
a wig,
and a dress.

I didn't expect much.
Maybe a caricature.
Something funny.
Something pang-katawanan lang.

But when Will finished…

When I looked into the mirror…

When I saw the version of me he created…

I froze.

I was beautiful.

Becoming Maria Kim

Not "pwede na."
Not "cute."
But genuinely… beautiful.

My cheekbones were snatched.
My lips were soft.
My eyes looked feminine and sweet.
The wig framed my face perfectly.

I didn't recognize myself—
and at the same time,
I did.

It felt like I was meeting the girl
I buried so long ago.

We did a photoshoot.
We posted the pictures on Facebook.

And suddenly—
I blew up.

Compliments everywhere.
Stunned reactions.
Messages.
Praise.

For the first time in years,
I felt seen again—
not because of pain,
not because of struggle,
but because of beauty.

Then I had an idea.
A crazy one.

What if I uploaded these photos
on the dating app?

I hesitated…
but the curiosity won.

The moment I posted the pictures—
my phone *exploded*.

Matches.
Messages.
Notifications.

And not random guys—
but hot men.
Muscular.
Tall.
Athletic.
Handsome.
Even married men.
Men I never thought would look at me twice.

Feminine beauty was adored in America.
It was a fantasy to many.
An obsession to some.
But rarely a pathway to real love.

Most of them wanted hookups.
Most wanted the fantasy.
Very few wanted the person behind the makeup.

And honestly?

I didn't care.
I was enjoying it.

For once,
I was the one being chased.

Admired.
Desired.

The validation healed a wound I didn't know I still had.

But among the floods of messages,
one stood out.

A simple profile.
A simple picture.
A simple smile.

And a simple greeting.

"Hello."

His name was **Marcus**.

I didn't know it yet,
but that single "Hello"
would change everything.

Not because he was handsome.
Not because he wanted me.
But because he would become a chapter
I never expected to write.

A chapter that would challenge me,
break me,
teach me,
and transform me.

It all began with that single word:

Hello.

(To be continued...)

CHAPTER SIXTEEN:

THE MAN I NEVER NOTICED — UNTIL THE NIGHT, I MET HIM

Marcus was never my type.

Filipinos grow up with a universal fantasy checklist:

Maputi.
Tall.
Blue eyes.
Troy Bolton from High School Musical.
Yung tipong pag nag-smile, may sound effect na *ting!*

But Marcus, in pictures?

He was Black — dark-skinned, soft-featured, with an average body.
Not muscular.
Not fair-skinned.
Not Disney prince material.
Not the type na makikita mo pa lang ay ma-in love ka na.

He looked simply.
Ordinary.
Quiet.

So naturally...
I didn't expect anything.

He was just another guy on a dating app.
Nice.
Polite.
But not exciting.

Until he proved me wrong.

Marcus was different.

Becoming Maria Kim

Really different.

He never sent dick pics.
He never sent videos.
He never made me feel like a fantasy.

He asked:

"How was your day?"
"Did you eat?"
"Are you adjusting okay?"

At a time when most men only messaged me for one thing,
Marcus messaged like he actually cared.

When he found out I had just moved in,
he offered to help me unpack.

I thought:

"Hala, ang bait naman neto.
Wala ko naanad ani."

But despite all that sweetness,
meeting him didn't happen.

Not because I didn't want to—
but because I was scared.

I was scared he wouldn't like the real me.
I was scared he'd compare me to the pictures.
I was scared to show up without Will's makeup magic.

Without Will, I felt ordinary again.
Makita ra akong pagka-lalaki.
Makita akong imperfections.

And Will couldn't glam me every time I went on a date—
he has his own dating life too.

So for weeks, Marcus and I messaged
like two people circling each other
but never colliding.

He even offered to swing by with his dog
"just so you know I'm not a crazy person."

But I said no.

Because without makeup...
I wasn't ready yet.

Then came the night everything changed.

I was at Leo's house with Allan and Marco.
Party, chika, laughter, alcohol —
the holy trinity of gay bonding.

I was tipsy.
Happy.
Loose enough to forget my fears.

Then Marcus messaged:

"What are you doing?"

I told him I was tipsy and planning to go home soon.

He replied:

**"It's not safe.
I'll pick you up."**

My heart stopped.

No one in my past ever cared about my safety.
No one ever picked me up.
No one ever showed up for me.

But Marcus?

He wanted to take care of me.

I told my friends and instantly—
emergency glam team mode.

"HOY! Ayuha na! He's coming!"

They dressed me up.
Blush here.
Contour there.
Lip gloss everywhere.

And the only wig available
was the platinum blonde one.

So there I was—

a budget version of Daenerys Targaryen
ready to conquer Westeros
pero cheap ang production.

But honestly?

I looked pretty.
A goddess—even on a budget.

I agreed to meet him.

Ten minutes later, a blue truck parked outside.

Marcus messaged:

"I'm here."

My friends chanted:

"GOOD LUCK, GIRL!"

Becoming Maria Kim

My wig prayed for its life.

I stepped outside,
heart pounding like a karaoke machine stuck on max volume.

And then—
there he was.

He stepped out of the truck wearing:

- checked long sleeves
- a bonnet
- jeans
- boots

Simple.
Soft-featured.
Comfortable in his own skin.
Warm.
Approachable.
Unexpectedly handsome in real life.

Tall enough.
Gentle enough.
Kind enough.

He smiled—
a small, shy, sweet smile
that hit me unexpectedly hard.

He walked toward me and said:

"Hi."

I panicked and blurted out:

"Sorry if I look ugly in person."

He laughed softly.
Not mocking.

Not rude.
Just warm.

And he said:

"You actually look prettier in person than in your pictures."

My knees almost gave up on me.
My wig almost resigned.

Then he extended his hand and said:

**"Marcus.
I'm glad we met."**

And just like that—

In the cold air,
under the streetlights,
with my blonde wig shaking for dear life,
and a gentle Black man smiling at me…

I realized:

**You don't have to be someone's fantasy
to be someone's choice.**

What I didn't know yet was this:

That night was only the beginning
of a story that would change me
in ways I never expected.

[To be continued…]

CHAPTER SEVENTEEN:

THE NIGHT THAT CHANGED EVERYTHING

When Marcus opened the truck door for me,
I swear I felt my soul float out of my body.

Chivalry is not dead —
it just came in the form of a soft-spoken Black man
with gentle eyes and an average build.

For the first time in my life,
someone treated me like a woman.
Not a secret.
Not a joke.
Not a fantasy.

But someone worth taking care of.

I slid into the seat feeling like a tipsy princess
with a bargain Daenerys wig,
and my heart was pounding
like a karaoke machine stuck on MAX VOLUME.

The ride was fast,
pero sa akong memory,
it was slow motion.

We talked easily.
We laughed.
No dead air.
No awkwardness.
Just... natural chemistry.

Before I knew it,
we were pulling into his apartment complex —
literally a sneeze away from mine.

Safe.
Warm.
Comfortable.

Inside, he asked if I wanted something to drink.
Of course, naka-"YES" ko
even if I was already tipsy from Leo's house.

We started talking more deeply.

Marcus was 35.
I was 30.
Six-year gap —
sakto ra.
Dili tiguwang.
Dili bata.
Perfect lang sa akong standards
nga dili ko ganahan mahimong caregiver sa akong uyab.

He had two kids and was legally married but separated.
His kids lived in another state.

My mind immediately went:

"Giatay na! Rebound na sad ko ani?"

Pero he kept talking...
and everything made sense.
He spoke with depth I didn't expect.

He was a veteran.
14 years in the military.
PTSD.
Emotional scars hidden behind a shy smile.

The Special Education teacher in me thought:

"Ah okay, kabalo ko unsaon ani."

Becoming Maria Kim

But at the same time,
I asked myself:

"Ngano concerned kaayo ko? Hook-up rani uy."

Then it happened.

Our lips collided.
Not planned.
Not awkward.
Not forced.

Just heat.
Chemistry.
Tension snapping like a rubber band ready to break.

He pressed me against the wall
like I was the hottest FHM cover model
and he was the soldier finally coming home from deployment.

His body responded quickly —
mas gahi pa sa bato.
Char!

It was one of the best kisses of my life.
Passionate.
Urgent.
Hungry.

And the whole time
I was terrified my wig would fall off.

Mga geng,
imagine if mahulog akong wig
and makit-an niya akong wig cap —
murag siyag nag-try og make love to an alien.

Luckily,
my wig stayed loyal that night.

We didn't go all the way.
Hoy, dili ko easy girl.
But enough happened
to release every tension
we both carried for weeks.

It was still dark outside
when I decided to go home.

I told him
I didn't want to stay overnight
because honestly —
I didn't know him enough
not to end up in a luggage
thrown somewhere in the New Mexico desert.

I don't want to be a Netflix documentary.
Pass ko diha.

I said I could just walk home.
Walking distance ra man.

But Marcus insisted.

**"No. I'll drive you.
I need to see you go inside safely."**

Mga geng…
GREEN. FLAG. KING.

Most men don't care after they get what they want.

But Marcus?
He cared enough to make sure I was safe.
He parked.
Watched me walk to my door.
Waited until I went in.

And seconds after I closed the door…
my phone buzzed.

Marcus:
I had fun tonight.
I hope to see you again.

And right there —
in my tiny apartment,
with my wig still barely holding on —
my heart whispered:

"Oh no…
here we go again."

[To be continued…]

CHAPTER EIGHTTEEN:

ALMOST, BUT NOT QUITE

Marcus and I continued seeing each other—
but we weren't exclusive.

We both stayed in the dating app,
both still checking messages,
both still talking to other people,
pero klaro kaayo:

We were each other's most consistent choice.

Every week, every few days,
somehow,
we always ended up with each other.

There was comfort.
Familiarity.
Softness.
Routine.

I spent most nights at his place.
We cooked together sometimes.
Sometimes he'd watch TV while I scrolled on my phone.
Sometimes I'd talk, he'd listen.
Sometimes he'd talk, and I'd try to decode him
because Marcus was a quiet man.

Not silent.
Just... peaceful.
Calm.
A man with his own rhythm.

His love language was service, I think.
He wouldn't say "I miss you,"
pero he'd bring me food.
He wouldn't say "you're beautiful,"

pero he'd fix the heater, clean the kitchen,
or make sure I got home safe.

He was not the type of man
who told you what you wanted to hear,
but always honest about what he felt.

In other words…

**He was the kind of man
dangerous to fall for
because he didn't give promises—
he gave actions.**

And let's not forget—

I WAS NOT TRANSITIONED YET.
Not fully.
Not even close.

Makeup?
Disaster.

Every time I tried, mura kog caricature sa newspaper.
Or mascot sa mall show sa Ayala.
I did not have the talent.
Liquid foundation, blush-on, lipstick —
pero I still looked like a clown
na gi-pressure to join Miss Q&A unprepared.

So most days,
I wore a wig,
lip tint,
and pure confidence.

Whenever we hung out,
naa ra jud mi sa balay.

I didn't question it.
I assumed:

"Maybe mauwaw siya makiglaag nako.
Lalaki iyang kuyog, naka-wig pa gyud.
Basig i-judge mi."

But one day,
Marcus surprised me.

"Let's go to the mall."

I froze.

HUH?
LIKE...
OUTSIDE?
IN PUBLIC?
WITH ME?
WITH MY WIG??

I told him:

"I don't have outfits for that.
And I don't know how to do my makeup.
Mura kog bagong tubo nga bayot sa Pilipinas."

He shrugged and said:

"It's fine."

And that small gesture?

It broke something open in me.

This wasn't just hanging out.
This felt like a date.

So there I was—

Skinny jeans.
Wig secured with a cap kay basin mahulog.
Tight shirt.
Praying to all saints
nga dili ko ma-expose in the middle of JCPenney.

The moment we walked inside the mall,
I felt something shift.

Marcus was walking beside me.
Not in front of me.
Not behind me.

Beside me.
Like a partner.
Like someone unafraid.

I felt safe.
Seen.
Almost claimed.

In that moment,
I thought:

"This is how couples act.
This is how boyfriend-girlfriend feels.
Maybe... this is it?"

Assumptions are dangerous—
but tell me,
what woman hasn't fallen for the "almost"?

We kept seeing each other.
Cooking.
Talking.
Kissing.
Sleeping side by side.
Texting every day.

But weeks passed
and he never asked me to be his.

And you know what impatient women do
when they can't wait anymore?

We ask first.

So, one night,
lying in my bed,
wig hung on the closet door like a silent witness,
I opened my phone.

Typed the message.

My heart pounding,
my throat dry,
my fingers trembling:

"Hey… what are we?
What's our score?"

I stared at the screen.
Waiting.
Overthinking.
Panicking.

This was the moment.

The truth.

The answer that could either
make my heart soar…

or break it quietly.

Marcus was typing.

Three dots appeared.

Disappeared.

Came back.

Disappeared again.

My heart dropped into my stomach.

And then—

the message arrived.

(To be continued...)

CHAPTER NINETEEN:

THE ANSWER THAT BROKE THE SPELL

Mura kog ga-atang sa Miss Universe coronation night, mga geng.
Kanang moment nga duha nalang naggunitay sa stage,
nag-ngisi pero nagtuo nga sila ang mudaog...

Ug kalit nalang si Steve Harvey mo-ingon ug:

"I have to apologize..."

ING-ANA KA KULBA.

My chest tightened.
My breath got shallow.
My stomach twisted into knots.

I felt like I was back on that beach in Camotes—
waiting for Jason to break my heart at 2am.

And finally...
the message came.

Marcus said:

**"I'm not ready for a relationship.
I like being around you...
but with everything happening in my life right now,
I'm not ready for you.
I need to find myself first.
I'm sorry if I gave you the wrong impression."**

In other words?

**GI-BUSTED KO.
AGAIN.
PUTANG INA.**

Becoming Maria Kim

Another chapter,
another heartbreak,
another "it's not you, it's me" bullshit.

And as much as I wanted to be mature about it,
the truth was—

Nasakitan ko.
Nasuko ko.
Nagtampo ko.

I texted him with a hurt heart:

"So, after those steamy nights...
katawan ko lang pala habol mo?
Why did you lead me on?
Why give me hope?"

There was silence.
Long, cold, punishing silence.

After that conversation...
everything became awkward.

Our chats slowed.
Then faded.
Then disappeared.

Until one day—
wala na.

No messages.
No calls.
No "good mornings."
No memes.
No "you home safe?"
No nothing.

Becoming Maria Kim

Dead air.
Dead end.
Dead hope.

I was devastated.

I tried talking to other men.
I entertained guys who messaged me on dating apps,
but honestly,
they were not even worthy of being compared to Marcus.

They didn't talk like him.
They didn't listen like him.
They didn't care like him.
They didn't look at me the way he did.

He wasn't perfect,
pero in my heart...

Marcus was "the one that could've been."

But life doesn't bend to our fantasies.
And if we force something that's not meant for us,
tayo rin ang madudurog.

So, I buried the almost-love with him.
Quietly.
Privately.
Painfully.

To distract myself,
I traveled.

Vegas.
California.
Colorado.
Utah.
Texas.
Arizona.

Becoming Maria Kim

I was chasing cities,
sceneries,
sunsets,
and the hope that in one of those places…

I would find another version of Marcus.
Someone who chooses me.
Someone real.
Someone ready.

Pero every city left me emptier.

Every state felt like an escape,
not a destination.

I was ready to surrender.
Ready to stop looking.
Ready to accept that maybe
love was not written for girls like me.

But life has a strange sense of humor.

Because just when I stopped searching…

Just when I told myself
that the universe had no more surprises for me…

Just like how my life always resets
every time I enter a new environment…

Someone else appeared.

Not in New Mexico.

But in Las Vegas.

A man named **Philip**.

Becoming Maria Kim

A love disguised as trauma.
A storm wearing a smile.
A lesson dressed like romance.

And I didn't know it yet...
but meeting Philip
would change the next part of my life
in a way I never saw coming.

[To be continued...]

CHAPTER TWENTY

LOVE, LIES, AND LAS VEGAS

Vegas arrived in my life the same way temptation always does—
loud, glittery, seductive, and perfectly timed when I was emotionally
broken.

It was COVID season,
everyone else was trying to survive,
and there I was—

trying to survive heartbreak
by hunting men like Pokémon.

My batchmates—Bern, Warly, Antolin, and Evina—were already
living in Vegas,
so I decided to visit them.

And by "visit," I mean:

free home.
free lodging.
free food.
free escape.

Plus, since I was working from home,
I could be anywhere.

And Vegas felt like the perfect hunting ground.

I dated men left and right.
So many that every night was a free dinner.
Buffet here.
Steakhouse there.
Wine on this night.
Sushi on the next.

Becoming Maria Kim

Mga geng,
I was in my **BITCH ERA.**

I was living my best hook-up revenge fantasy,
trying to forget Marcus
and trying to fill the void he left behind.

And then…

Philip happened.

A man who didn't just take me on a date—
he took me on an **all-expense-paid experience.**

Airport pickup.
Hotel stay.
Fine dining.
Road trips.
Shopping.

I was shocked.

Sauna,
ako ang sponsor sa lalaki.
Ako ang nagbabayad ng milk tea,
ako ang nagdadala ng Jollibee,
ako ang nagpapalabas ng sweldo.

Pero this time?

Ako ang prininsesa.

Trips continued.
Shopping sprees.
Expensive restaurants.
Weekend getaways.

But like every shiny object in Vegas…

there was a price.
And the price was trauma.

It happened on a birthday trip to San Francisco.

We were lying on the hotel bed,
lights dim,
him scrolling on his phone…

when I saw it.

A heart emoji.
Then another.
Then another.

Notifications popping up like taunts.

Not for me.
Not from me.

My stomach dropped.

Something was wrong.

He slept eventually.
But I didn't.

Instead,
I memorized his phone passcode
like a CIA agent trained by heartbreak.

And when I finally had the chance—
when he went to shower,
when the room fell silent,
and only my heartbeat kept time…

I opened his phone.

And there it was.

The truth.
Unfiltered.
Undeniable.

Long sweet messages.
Heart emojis.
Love notes.
Good mornings.
Good nights.
"Miss you."
"Can't wait to see you."
"My heart still belongs to you."

All sent to his **ex.**

And the worst part?

My competition was not just any girl—
but a fully transitioned trans woman.

Beautiful.
Retokada.
May suso.
May curves.
May glow-up.
May confidence.

Layo kaayo ko niya.
I felt like a budget version of her.

And yes—
we were already official when this happened.

I froze.
Namugnaw ko mga geng.
I didn't know what to feel.
What to say.
How to breathe.

Another failure.
Another heartbreak.
Another humiliation.

But I didn't react.
Not yet.

Because this time,
I wanted control.

This time,
I wanted the ending.

This time,
I wanted to deliver a lesson
he would NEVER forget.

My application to move to Vegas was already in process.
I really thought he was serious,
that maybe he was my fresh start.

But no.

He gave me betrayal instead.

And betrayal?

That deserves a plot twist.

So, I planned my exit with grace…
and vengeance.

No confrontation.
No drama.
No shouting.
No crying.

I acted normal.
I smiled.
I laughed.
I pretended nothing was wrong.

He booked our Hawaii trip.
He paid for the resort.
The activities.
The tours.
Everything.

We shopped for outfits.
Matching colors pa.
Like newlyweds going on a honeymoon.

But deep inside me?

I was sharpening the knife.

Not literal, ha.
Pero emotionally?

I was preparing the coldest revenge I ever served.

When the day of the Hawaii trip arrived...

I did not show up.

Not even a shadow.

No text.
No explanation.
No goodbye.
No trace.

I blocked him everywhere.

I left him confused, broken, humiliated.

And as I sat there,
bags packed to leave Vegas,
I told myself:

**"Hindi ko deserved ang betrayal mo.
Ngayon, matitikman mo ang higanti ng pinagluruan."**

It was poetic.
It was savage.
It was teleserye.
And honestly?

It was satisfying.

I was still broken, yes.
But for once in my life...

my heartbreak came with justice.

A dish best served cold—
and I served it like frozen dessert in the afterlife.

[To be continued...]

CHAPTER TWENTY-ONE:

THE BUS RIDE, THE BREAKDOWN, AND THE MESSAGE THAT CHANGED EVERYTHING

The brave version of me—the fierce Kim who could cut men with a
single eyebrow raise—
that version was gone.

What was left was the quiet, breaking version of me
riding a twenty-four–hour bus back to Albuquerque
like a dramatic indie film nobody asked for.

I wanted to go home immediately.
I didn't want to breathe the same Las Vegas air for another second.
I searched flights.
All expensive.
All fully booked.

Pota.
Kung kelan pa ako nagmamadaling umuwi,
saka naman naging mayaman ang presyo ng mga flights.

So I took the bus.

And maybe that was destiny—
because the universe wanted me to sit with my pain.
To look out the window and face the truth I kept running from.

The scenery passed like a montage.
Long roads.
Gas stations glowing at night.
Mountains hiding in the dark.
The hum of the engine vibrating through my chest.

And there I was...
a trans girl in a wig,
heartbroken again,
hugging my bag in silence,

naiiyak,
nag-eemote,
habang nagpa-party ang heartbreak ko sa loob ng bus.

Every song hit differently.
Every lyric felt like a prophecy.

And suddenly, I realized something…

**Maybe the reason why men never take me seriously
is because I'm not taking myself seriously either.
I am still hiding behind a wig.
A costume.
A temporary identity.**

Maybe…
just maybe…

it's time to fully become the woman I was always meant to be.

So right there, in that cold bus seat,
with tear stains drying on my cheeks,
I made a decision that would change my entire life:

**I will transition.
Fully.
Completely.
Fearlessly.**

I will grow my hair.
Change my wardrobe.
Take hormones.
Learn makeup.
Rediscover myself.

I will glow up so hard
that every man who treated me like a clown
will regret the day they underestimated me.

For the first time in years…
I felt hope.

I felt purpose.

I felt certainty.

I whispered to myself:

"This time, I will become who I really am."

And just as I was embracing that quiet promise—
just as I was wiping the last tear from my eyelash—
my phone buzzed.

A notification.

Not from Philip.
Not from another man from Vegas.
Not from anyone I expected.

I looked at the screen.

Marcus.

A message from the man I thought was gone from my life.

A message from someone who once held my heart gently.

A message from someone who saw me
not as a fantasy,
not as a wig,
not as a body,
but as a person.

"Him?"
I whispered to myself.

A part of me froze.

Another part broke open.

Another part of me hoped again—
the dangerous kind of hope you feel when someone from your past
reappears...

And right there,
on that long, dark bus ride,
my entire life shifted direction again—

toward a man
I wasn't done loving.

[To be continued...]

CHAPTER TWENTY-TWO:

DELIVERED TO THE ALTAR OF ANOTHER LIFE

There he was—
Marcus, leaning against his familiar blue truck,
parked outside the Albuquerque bus station
like a scene from a movie I wasn't sure I wanted to watch again.

He waved at me, soft and warm, like nothing ever happened.
Like he didn't reject me.
Like I didn't cry over him.
Like we were just... us.

While I was still on the bus,
he had asked me how I was, how life was treating me.
I told him everything—
Philip, the betrayal, the emojis, the heartbreak, the revenge.

He didn't judge me.

He didn't say "I told you so."

Instead, he said he was sorry.
Sorry I was hurt.
Sorry someone treated me that way.
Sorry I had to go through that alone.

And he offered to pick me up because
"that's the least I can do."

I didn't look at him romantically in that moment.
Not at all.
Not after everything.

I saw him as a kind man—
someone who appears at the exact moment you need a soft place to
land.

He carried my luggage onto the back of his truck,
opened the passenger door for me,
and drove us through the cold Albuquerque night.

Inside the truck, it was quiet—
the kind of quiet that doesn't demand anything.

Then he spoke.
Gentle.
Warm.
Reassuring in a way that disarmed every defense I tried to rebuild.

"You don't deserve what happened," he said.
"You deserve someone who chooses you."

I didn't know whether to laugh or cry.
Maybe both.

When he wrapped his arms around me later that night,
I let myself collapse for a moment.
I was weak.
I was hurting.
And his body felt like a place I once called home.

Two bodies coming together—
not out of desperation,
not out of lust,
but out of familiarity,
memory,
and the kind of comfort that only exists
between two people who cared for each other
but never quite figured out how to love each other properly.

It felt magical.
But also dangerous.
Because magic never lasts.

We slipped into a rhythm again—
something like a relationship,
something like a healing space,
something like a soft landing.

Marcus made me meals.
Checked on me.
Called me over.
Kept me close.

I found myself more in his apartment than my own.

But one day,
curiosity whispered too loudly inside my head.

I glanced at his phone
and saw her name—
the ex he once told me he wasn't ready to let go of.

They were messaging again.

I froze.

Not in jealousy.
Not in anger.
But in recognition.

This felt like another Philip.

So, I didn't hope.
Not anymore.

I didn't cry.
Not this time.

I simply accepted the truth—
maybe he cares about me,

maybe he wants me near,
maybe he feels something…

…but maybe I wasn't the woman he was ready to choose.

And strangely,
I didn't resent him for that.

Despite everything,
we became official.

But unlike before,
I wasn't exploding with excitement.
Wala na ang fireworks.
Wala na ang fairy-tale expectations.
Wala na ang "Marcus will save me" narrative.

I knew he was still texting his ex.
I knew he was still unsure.
I knew our time had an expiration date.

Pero sige lang.

Maybe he realized I was better.
Maybe he was trying.
Maybe he was healing too.

And maybe…
maybe this was enough.

Besides,
I didn't expect our relationship to last.

Why?

Because stupid Philip made me apply for Vegas,
and I had already resigned from my school.

Becoming Maria Kim

My plans were set in motion,
and I couldn't undo them anymore.

I told myself:

"If this works, fine.
If not, I'm done being desperate."

When we finally reached Vegas,
when Marcus carried my bags like he always did,
when he walked me to the entrance of my new place…

…it didn't feel like an ending.
It felt like a pause.

He stood there quietly, hands in his pockets,
looking at me like he wanted to say something
but didn't know how.

I felt it too—
that strange pull between us,
that soft awareness that whatever we had
wasn't finished.
Not really.

He helped me place my things by the door,
giving small instructions I pretended not to listen to
just so I could hear his voice longer.

Then he hugged me.

A long, warm, familiar hug—
not goodbye,
not see-you-soon,
but something in-between.
Something that didn't have a name.

When he pulled away,
he gave me that soft half-smile of his,

eyes lingering a second too long
before he looked away.

"Text me when you're settled," he said.

Simple words.
But they carried weight.
Promise.
Possibility.
Uncertainty.

I watched him walk back to his blue truck.
Watched him pause before opening the door.
Watched him look at me one more time.

And in that moment,
I couldn't help but ask myself:

Is this really the end of us?
Or are we just beginning again
in a different city,
at a different time,
as different versions of ourselves?

I didn't know.
He didn't know.

But something in my chest whispered:

"This isn't over."

Not yet.
Maybe not ever.

[To be continued...]

CHAPTER TWENTY-THREE:

THE BIRTH OF MARIA KIM

The moment Marcus drove out of Vegas and disappeared into the road,
I made a decision:

This time, the love story I was going to fight for was my own.

No more wigs.
No more costumes.
No more pretending.

Just me—
the woman I had been hiding for years.

Transitioning wasn't a fantasy anymore.
It wasn't a joke, or a dare, or a plan I whispered to myself in moments of heartbreak.

It was real.
It was happening.

I started wearing women's clothes everywhere—
not just at home, not just with friends,
but out in public.

My hair was longer now.
My confidence?
Even longer.

I learned what silhouettes flattered my frame.
I knew what colors made me glow.
I practiced makeup until I could finally say:

"Wow...
this is really me."

Becoming Maria Kim

No more wig to hide behind.
No more "Kenneth" mask to wear.
No more diluted version of myself.

For the first time in my life,
I wasn't pretending to be a woman.

I was becoming one.

But there was one problem.

The school that hired me in Vegas?
They hired **Kenneth**.

All my documents, my interviews, my forms—
everything said *Mr. Bongabong*.

And now,
here I was,
showing up as Maria Kim.

I had a full debate with myself:

- Should I stay as Kenneth at work?

- Should I wait longer?

- What if they say no?

- What if they fire me?

- What if they don't accept me?

I was running out of time.
We were scheduled to report the following morning.

The clock was ticking.

Becoming Maria Kim

So, I gathered everything—
my courage,
my fear,
my hope,
my heart—
and I wrote an email:

A letter telling the principal who I truly was,
who I wanted to be addressed as,
and how I wanted to start my new life
as **Maria Kim**.

I hit send.

And there was silence.

No reply.

No reassurance.

Nothing.

I barely slept that night.
Every scenario ran through my mind:

"What if they fire me?"
"What if this is the end of my career?"
"What if I'm forced to be Kenneth again?"

I hated how terrified I felt.
But at the same time, this fear proved something:

I was no longer willing to hide.
Even if it cost me everything.

The next day came.

Becoming Maria Kim

I dressed safely—
androgynous,
neutral,
subtle.
No makeup.
Just enough to breathe,
enough to pass,
enough to protect myself
if the worst happened.

When I arrived at the school,
my heart was pounding like a drum inside my chest.

Then my phone buzzed.

The principal wanted to see me.

Shit.
This was it.

This was the moment I thought my entire future would collapse.

I walked into his office,
hands cold,
throat tight,
ready for the worst.

But he smiled.

A warm smile.

A welcoming smile.

And he said—

"Good morning, Kim."

I froze.

Did I hear that right?

Becoming Maria Kim

Then he continued:

"I'm sorry for not replying immediately.
I didn't want you to panic.
But I want you to know—we fully support you.
I have already informed the staff,
and all our records have been updated to Ms. Kim."

I felt my knees weaken.

He changed my directory.
My email.
My title.
My identity in the system.

He even said,
"We're glad you're here."

I walked out of that office
feeling like the universe finally opened a door
after years of forcing myself through windows.

That was the day
Maria Kim was born.

Not in shame.
Not in hiding.
Not in secrecy.

But in full view of the world—
validated,
recognized,
respected.

This was my era.

My transition.
My rebirth.
My freedom.

No more shrinking.
No more apologizing.
No more pretending.

From this moment on—

I will be seen.
I will be loved.
I will be brave.
And I will live as the woman
I was always meant to become.

This is Maria Kim.
And no force in the world can stop her now.

CHAPTER TWENTY-FOUR:

THE RICE, THE REVEAL, AND FERNANDO

I was finally living the dream.

Not pretending.
Not hiding.
Not half-woman, half-wig.

Just **Kim.**
A woman.
Seen.
Acknowledged.
Respected.

At work, everyone called me "she."
In public, no one stared.
In malls, I walked with confidence.
In grocery stores, I bought my shampoo from the women's aisle
without shame or hesitation.

It felt like I had been a woman my whole life—
just waiting for the world to catch up.

One ordinary day, I went grocery shopping.
Rice was on my list.
Of course it was—
rice is life for Filipinos,
even in the land of burritos.

Pero bakit naman kasi nilalagay ang bigas
sa pinaka-itaas ng aisle?
Ano to, CrossFit challenge?

Becoming Maria Kim

I tiptoed, stretched, practically climbed the shelf,
pero wa jud—
di maabot.

And just as I was about to accept my fate as a rice-less woman,
someone suddenly spoke behind me.

"Do you need help?"

I turned around.

Mexican guy.
Cute.
Chubby in a cuddly way.
Soft eyes.
Clean haircut.
Friendly smile.

Pero honestly?
I didn't care about any of that.

All I wanted was my sack of rice.

So I said, "Yes please,"
and he reached it effortlessly like it weighed nothing.

"Thank you," I said, ready to continue my grocery list.

But then...

"Can I get your number?"

HA?
SCAM?
SURVEY?
HUMAN TRAFFICKING?

Never in my life—
as Kenneth or Kim—
did a man in public ask for my number like that.

I blinked.
Twice.

"I'm sorry… what did you need?"
I asked, just to confirm na tama ba ako ng dinungog.

"Your number," he repeated.
"You're really pretty.
I didn't want to miss the chance."

SYET.

Nagloko akong kalibutan.

Naga fireworks sa ceiling.
Naga best actress akong puso.
Naga slow motion akong buhok.

Pretty daw ako.
PRETTY.

Dili "you look nice."
Dili "cute ka."
PRETTY.

Ni-ana ko sa akong self internally:

Giatay. Ning ana nako ka gwapa?

And because I was suddenly Anne Curtis,
I did what any feeling-maganda girl would do—

I gave him my number.

Should I have done that?
Probably not.
Stranger danger.
Kidnapping era.
Possible documentary sa Netflix.

Pero syempre sa moment na 'yon,
I was like:

"Char! Bigay ko na. Baka destiny."

I continued my grocery shopping
with a little more sway in my hips
and a little more confidence in my heart.

I felt PRETTY.
GORGEOUS.
UNSTOPPABLE.

*"Pag mohumok akong buhok... my God,
mahiwi gyud ang mga lalaki sa akoa."*

Pag-uwi ko, I unpacked my groceries,
ready to forget the whole thing
kasi wala man nag-text.

POTA.
Pinaasa lang ko.
Ginamit lang akong kagwapohan to reach the rice?

Then—

DING.

Text from an unknown number.

"Hi."

Syempre I replied:

"Who is this?"

One second.
Two seconds.
Three seconds.

Then the next message came:

"This is the guy you met at the grocery store.
My name is Fernando."

And just like that—

my glow-up era
finally had its first suitor.

[To be continued...]

CHAPTER TWENTY-FIVE:

THE MAN WHO LOVED ME FIRST

Fernando and I had been exchanging messages for days. He wasn't the only one—I was still entertaining a few men here and there—but Fernando stood out. He was consistent, respectful, and proper. Most men I met wanted a home run right after dinner, expecting me to be dessert.
Pero syempre, hindi tayo easy girl.

Fernando was different. He messaged me good morning, asked how my day was, told me stories about his work, and remembered little details I didn't even think mattered. There was a gentleness about him... the kind I used to feel with Marcus.

I have to admit, I wasn't physically attracted to him. Not like how I was to Marcus. But Fernando had something else—**security**, **kindness**, and a heart that wasn't trying to use me.

He eventually asked me out on a date.

I said yes.

He took me to an Italian restaurant his family loved. The place was warm, intimate, the kind of restaurant where couples share secrets over candlelight. He opened doors for me, pulled my chair, listened when I talked, and never—not even once—made a move that felt disrespectful.

It was sweet.
Maka-kilig.

Our second date came. Still no pressure. Still no rushing. Still that gentle smile and patience that I wasn't used to.

Then our third date happened—a short day trip outside Vegas.
We laughed.

We shared stories.
We talked about family, dreams, future plans.

Pero kahit masaya...
wala pa ring spark.

I tried to convince myself maybe it would come later.
Maybe attraction was something that could grow.
Maybe kindness was a better foundation than butterflies.

Then, somewhere between the long drive and the golden desert sunset, Fernando turned to me—hands slightly shaking, eyes soft but certain—and said:

"Will you be my girlfriend?"

My heart stopped.

Not from kilig.

But from confusion.

Because deep inside me was a name I couldn't shake:

Marcus.

And saying yes felt like cheating on a feeling I still wasn't over.

I hesitated.
I really did.
My chest tightened, my hands got cold, and for a moment I wanted to run.

But Fernando looked at me with so much sincerity it almost broke me.

He was a good man.
A kind man.
A man who treated me exactly how I wished Marcus had treated me.

So I told myself:

Becoming Maria Kim

Maybe love doesn't always start with fireworks.
Maybe some loves are slow-burning.
Maybe I can learn to love him.
Hindi naman mahirap mahalin ang mabait.

I said,
"Yes."

Fernando's face lit up like a child seeing fireworks for the first time.
He held my hand the whole ride back.
He kept glancing at me like he couldn't believe it.
Like he had won something precious.

And I smiled...
but inside, something felt missing.

We became inseparable—movies, dinners, sleepovers, late-night talks.
But every time he held my hand...

Marcus still haunted the back of my mind.

I hated myself for it.
I felt like a thief stealing Fernando's love without giving him the same amount back.
He adored me.
I was his world.
But I was only halfway there.

I tried.
God knows I tried.

But I couldn't distinguish if what I felt toward him was love...

...or pity.

And for that part of my life—
the part where I stayed even when half my heart was somewhere

else—
I will forever regret it.

Fernando deserved a full heart...
and I only gave him a broken one.

CHAPTERTWENTY-SIX:

THE PROPOSAL I NEVER SAW COMING

We were official.
Finally.

We posted the photos, changed the statuses, smiled for the world to see.
My friends spammed heart reactions and "about time!" comments.
My inbox buzzed like crazy.

But one message stopped me cold.

It came from someone who had been with me since college—
one of my closest friends,
one of the very few people who knew the real me from the beginning.

She congratulated me warmly,
then followed it with news I'd been waiting years to hear:

She was getting married.

My heart leaped.
We had dreamed of this since we were students—
me hosting her wedding,
standing beside her on her big day,
laughing at how far life had brought us.

I was ready to ask for the date, the venue, the theme…

But before I could type anything, she messaged:

"Geng… I'm sorry."

Sorry?

For what?

Then she told me.

Her fiancé…
didn't want me at the wedding.

Not because the budget was tight.
Not because the venue was small.
Not because we drifted apart.

But because—

I was transgender.

He was worried I might "attract attention."
That guests might "look at me differently."
That people might judge.
That I "might not look enough like a woman yet."

As if my existence would ruin their perfect day.

I forced myself to respond lightly.
I said I understood.
I told her it was okay.
I wished her happiness.

And the moment the chat ended…

I broke.

I cried so hard my chest hurt.
All the confidence I built,
all the bravery I learned,
all the transformations I worked for—
collapsed in one message.

Suddenly I saw myself through the eyes of people who didn't know
me:

Unwelcome.
Unacceptable.

Embarrassing.
Out of place.
Someone worth hiding.

"Am I really that disgusting?"
"A clown?"
"Dapat ba talaga akong ikahiya?"
"Is this all people will ever see of me?"

I cried like I was sixteen again,
like the world had pushed me back into a box I fought so hard to
escape.

And then—

my phone rang.

It was Fernando.

He heard my breathing—shaky, uneven, broken.
He didn't ask questions.
He didn't wait for an explanation.

He just said,
"I'm coming."

Fifteen minutes later, he was at our doorstep.
Hair messy, breath catching,
holding flowers and chocolates like the leading man in a romance
film.

He rushed inside the moment I opened the door.
He took one look at my face—red, swollen, trembling—
and pulled me into his arms.

I cried into his chest and told him everything—
the rejection, the shame, the humiliation.

"I wasn't even given a chance," I whispered.
"I'm not good enough even for a seat. Even for a moment."

Becoming Maria Kim

Fernando held my face gently,
wiped my tears with his thumb,
and looked straight into my soul.

Then he said the most unexpected,
most earth-shattering words
I had ever heard from a man:

"If they don't want you in their wedding...
then I'll give you a wedding where *YOU* are the one everyone
celebrates.
Kim... you won't just attend a wedding someday.
You will walk down the aisle in your own.
With *me* waiting at the end."

My breath caught.
My world went still.
My heart—after being crushed moments before—
suddenly fluttered with something I couldn't name.

Shock.
Hope.
Fear.
Surrender.
Love?
Maybe.
Not yet.
But something powerful.

For the first time in my life...
someone wasn't just choosing me in secret—
or behind closed doors—
or under the cover of darkness.

Someone was choosing me
loudly, proudly, fully, forever.

And in that moment...
the girl who was rejected from a wedding
was given a promise of her own.

A promise she never expected.
A promise she never believed she would ever hear.

A promise that would change the rest of her life.

CHAPTER TWENTY-SEVEN:

THE WEDDING I WALKED INTO WITH HALF A HEART

Everything happened so fast.
Too fast.
Parang whirlwind na hindi ko na nasabayan ang pag-ikot.

One day, Fernando was simply the man who helped me reach the
rice on the top shelf.
The next day, I was being introduced to his entire family—
their smiles too wide, their hugs too warm, their hopes too high.
His mother was already giving us her blessing, telling us how excited
she was,
already imagining our future together.

Then came the wedding plans.

I thought it was just us talking about the future.
Pero hindi.
His sister was asking for gown inspirations.
His cousins were planning the bachelor party.
His friends were telling him, "She's the one, bro."

And before I even fully processed anything…

…Fernando took me back to the place where we had our first date
and got down on one knee.

A public proposal.
People clapping.
Lights.
Phones recording.
A small ring box.
And a man looking at me like I was the biggest blessing of his life.

I said yes.
Not because my heart screamed it—
but because his eyes were pleading, hopeful, overflowing.

Becoming Maria Kim

We posted the announcement.
It spread like wildfire.

My family was thrilled.
His family embraced me whole-heartedly.
Friends congratulated us with long paragraphs and emojis.

Everyone was happy.

Except me.

I didn't know if I was happy because I was getting married…
or because I had fulfilled a fantasy I carried since childhood.

But something was missing.
A spark.
A fullness.
A truth.

I wasn't completely in love with my groom.

I loved the idea of the wedding—
the dress,
the aisle,
the validation,
the redemption arc—
but not the love story that was supposed to come with it.

It felt unfair.
Unfair to him.
Unfair to me.

But how could I break the heart of the man who helped repair mine
when I didn't even know how to repair my own?

I told myself maybe…
just maybe…
I would learn to love him after the wedding.

Becoming Maria Kim

People said love could grow.
So maybe mine would too.

The day of the wedding arrived.

I sat in front of the mirror—
my hair done,
my face glowing,
the dress hugging every curve of the woman I fought to become.

I looked at my reflection for a long time.

"You made it, Kim."

From sleeping on a classroom floor...
to walking down the aisle as a bride.

Life was unpredictable.
Beautiful.
Cruel.
Surreal.

But as I stared at myself—
perfect yet trembling—
a soft, unwelcome ache tugged at my chest.

Doubt.

A whisper I tried to silence.

Are you doing the right thing?
Is this love... or loneliness?
Is this marriage... or escape?

Before I could answer,
my phone buzzed.

I smiled a bit, expecting:

"Congrats, Kim!"
"You look stunning!"
"We're on our way!"

But when I checked the screen...

...I froze.

It was a call.

From him.

A voice I hadn't heard in so long,
but one my heart could never forget.

Marcus.

The man I once loved—
and maybe, in some quiet corner of my heart, still did.

My hands trembled.
My breath caught.

And on the day, I was supposed to promise forever to another man...

...the ghost of the man I wished had chosen me
was suddenly calling.

My phone kept vibrating on the table where my bouquet rested.
I glanced at the screen...

Marcus.

My heart dropped to my stomach.

For a moment, I froze.
My hands turned cold, my breath caught halfway in my chest.

Why now?
Why today?
Why on the one day I desperately needed peace?

Becoming Maria Kim

It took a few rings before I finally found the courage to answer.
My fingers were trembling.
My throat was tight.

I wasn't ready.

I wasn't ready for the past to call me
on the day I was supposed to secure my future.

I pressed the green button.

"Hello..."

Just that single word—
his voice, soft and familiar—
was enough to pull every memory out of the grave.
My knees weakened.
My chest tightened.

His hello felt like home...
and I hated myself for it.

"Hi," he said again. "How are you?"

How am I?
I'm in a wedding gown.
Mascara barely dry.
About to marry a man who loves me...
while the man I loved first is calling me.

He continued talking.
He said he was sorry.
That he needed time.
That he wasn't ready back then.
That he had been thinking about his life.

Every word stabbed a part of me I thought was already numb.

Becoming Maria Kim

Why did it take you this long?
Why call now?
Why today?

I swallowed hard.

"Marcus... I'm getting married today."

There was silence.

A silence so sharp
it cut through my veil
and straight into my heart.

"Oh," he finally said.

That one syllable shattered me.

Not because he didn't beg me to come back—
but because a part of me STILL wished he did.

Even if it would ruin everything.

Even if it would break Fernando.

Even if it would expose me as the mess I've always been.

But Marcus...
Marcus has never been selfish.

He didn't ask me to run.
He didn't ask me to choose him.
He didn't ask for anything.

He just breathed, painfully slow, and said—

"We can still be friends, right?"

Friends.
Putang ina.
FRIENDS?

Becoming Maria Kim

I wanted to scream.
To throw the phone.
To shout, *"Why only now? Why not when I was begging for you before?"*

But my voice betrayed me.

"Of course," I whispered.

When I ended the call, my hands were shaking so bad I almost dropped the phone.
Inside my chest?
A storm.

Ang daming mura na tumakbo sa isip ko.
Ang daming "what if."
Ang daming "sana."

But none of that mattered.

Not anymore.

My wedding coordinator knocked on the door.

"Kim… it's time."

I held my bouquet.
Took a breath so deep it hurt.

And when the doors opened,
and the music began,
and everyone stood up to look at me…

I forgot Marcus.

For the first time since morning—
my heart stopped hurting.

The lights, the flowers, the whispers…
The world blurred except for the aisle in front of me.

And for a moment—
a single, fragile moment—

I felt beautiful.
Beautiful enough to be a bride.
Beautiful enough to be chosen.
Beautiful enough to believe that maybe...
just maybe...

this could still be my happy ending.

Becoming Maria Kim

Everyone was looking at me while *Beautiful in White* played softly in the background. Cameras flashed. Phones rose like a sea of stars. My family back home was watching through a livestream, crying happy tears in the Philippines while I walked slowly down an aisle thousands of miles away.

And for the first time in my life, I felt it —
I was the most beautiful woman in the world.

My gown shimmered under the lights. My bouquet trembled in my hands. People whispered my name with admiration. The girl who once begged to be loved... now looked like a dream every little child wishes to become.

Then my eyes met Fernando.

There he was — the man who never left me.
The man who picked me up when I was crying.
The man who said he would give me a wedding better than the one I was excluded from.
The man who loved me without hesitation, without fear, without shame.

And in that moment, I told myself:
This is it. I am going to be Mrs.

The ceremony was beautiful. Romantic. Pinterest-worthy.
His mother — who had entire Pinterest boards dedicated to our wedding — cried the moment she saw me.
Our families celebrated.
Our friends cheered.
Strangers complimented our love story.

It was everything a girl could ever dream of... at least on the surface.

When the reception ended and the lights dimmed, we went home — husband and wife. Newly married. Supposedly the happiest night of our lives.

Becoming Maria Kim

Pero bakit ganon?

Pagkahiga namin ni Fernando sa kama…
habang nakayakap siya sa akin…
habang ramdam ko ang heartbeat niya sa likod ko…
parang may kulang. Parang may mali.

Because all I could hear in my head was Marcus' voice.
His "hello."
His "I hope you're okay."
His "we can still be friends."
His existence.

And right there, lying beside my husband on the very night of our
wedding, guilt stabbed me so deep I couldn't breathe.

Ang sama kong tao.
I was the worst woman alive.

How could I be here—
in the arms of a man who loved me completely,
while a part of my heart still reached out for someone else?

Fernando didn't deserve this.
He didn't deserve a half-present wife.
He didn't deserve someone who walked into a marriage with doubts
tucked beneath her veil.
He didn't deserve someone na may iniisip pang iba on their wedding
night.

I stared at the ceiling, tears quietly rolling down the sides of my face
so he wouldn't see.

Regret twisted in my chest like a knife.

If only I wasn't pressured.
If only I didn't rush things.
If only I listened to my heart instead of my fears.

If only I allowed myself to heal before choosing someone who chose me.

But now it was too late.

I turned to my side slowly, looking at Fernando sleeping peacefully beside me—
the man who would give the world just to keep me safe and loved.

And in that moment, I whispered silently in the dark:

"I'm sorry. You don't deserve a love that's incomplete."

And I prayed — not for myself...
but for him.

That one day, even if I fail him...
even if I break him...
he would still find someone who can love him the way he once loved me —
fully, fearlessly, and without the ghost of another man haunting their heart.

CHAPTER TWENTY-EIGHT:

THE DAYS AFTER "I DO"

Marriage did not change everything overnight.
In fact, it changed nothing at first.

Life continued the same way—
work in the morning,
conversation at night,
quiet dinners,
shared laughter,
shared space.

Only now… we had rings on our fingers.

Fernando was happy.
I could see it in the way he smiled when he woke up beside me.
In the way he held my hand in public.
In the way he proudly introduced me as his wife.

And I smiled too.
I tried.
God knows I tried.

But deep inside, guilt followed me like a shadow.

Some nights, Fernando would fall asleep first.
I would stay awake, staring at the ceiling, replaying everything in my
head:

Marcus' voice.
My wedding vows.
The way Fernando looked at me with so much certainty.
The way I looked at him with so much doubt.

I hated myself for that.

I asked myself every night:

"What kind of woman marries a man while still carrying the ghost of another?"
"What kind of wife starts a marriage with secrets inside her chest?"

And yet... I stayed quiet.

Fernando deserved peace.
And I convinced myself that my silence was kindness.

But silence is not honesty.
And kindness built on deception always has an expiration date.

Learning How to Be a Wife

I learned to cook meals he liked.
I learned to memorize his schedules.
I learned when he wanted silence
and when he wanted stories.

I learned to be a wife.

From the outside, we were perfect.

A Filipino trans woman and a devoted husband.
New life.
New beginning.
A romance people rooted for.

But inside me...
I was building a house on cracks.

I kept waiting for something to click.
For love to finally settle in the way everyone promised.

"You'll learn to love him," they said.
"Real love is chosen," they said.

So I chose every day.

I chose to stay.
I chose to try.
I chose to hope.

But the heart doesn't always follow logic.

The First Sign of Distance

It started with small things.

Fernando noticed I was quieter than usual.
That I took longer showers.
That I stayed up later.

"Are you just tired?" he asked.

I nodded.
"Work."

Another lie added to the pile.

He noticed I hugged him less.
He noticed I flinched when my phone vibrated.
He noticed when my smile didn't reach my eyes.

But he never accused me.

He only loved me harder.

And that was the part that broke me the most.

The Question That Almost Broke the Marriage

One night, as we were lying in bed, Fernando asked quietly:

"Kim… do you still love me?"

There was no anger in his voice.
Only fear.

My chest tightened.

I wanted to scream the truth.
I wanted to confess everything.
I wanted to beg for forgiveness before I even knew what I was sorry for.

But I looked at his eyes—
the same eyes that chose me in a world that once rejected me—

and I answered…

"Yes."

It was a soft lie.
A necessary lie.
A lie that saved the night.

But every lie costs something.

And I felt the payment slowly collecting.

Somewhere Else, the Past Was Still Breathing

I did not know then…
that somewhere, in a different city, in a different life,

Marcus was still thinking of me too.

I thought the wedding had finally closed that chapter.

I was wrong.

Because some love does not die.
It just waits.

And when it returns,
it never knocks gently.

CHAPTER TWENTY-NINE:

THE LOVE I CHOSE, THE MARRIAGE I LOST**

Days passed, and the distance between Fernando and me grew
wider.
Slow at first.
Subtle.
Quiet.

While my marriage was quietly unraveling...
my connection with Marcus, on the other hand, was growing deeper.

Even before everything fell apart between Fernando and me, I had
already noticed the signs.
He was talking to his ex-again.
Then it got worse.

One night, I saw dating apps on his phone.

And strangely...
I didn't confront him.

Because how could I, when my own heart was already somewhere
else?

It became an unspoken understanding between us—
we were both slipping away from the marriage in different
directions.

Fernando was seeing other people for distraction.
I was seeing someone for love.

And that someone... was Marcus.

A Marriage That Quietly Ended

Our home slowly stopped feeling like a home.

Becoming Maria Kim

We no longer slept in the same bed.
We no longer shared late-night conversations.
We no longer asked how each other's day went.

We lived like roommates.
Polite.
Distant.
Careful not to hurt what was already breaking.

Then one day, everything finally became clear.

I came home unexpectedly…
and there was another woman in the house.

There was no screaming.
No fighting.
No throwing of words like knives.

Just silence.

We sat down like two adults who already knew the ending of their story.

And with tired voices, we admitted the truth:

We were done.

Not because of anger.
Not because of hate.
But because we were both already gone.

That was the day my marriage officially ended—
not with drama…
but with acceptance.

Choosing Marcus, Fully and Finally

As Fernando and I drifted apart,
Marcus and I moved closer.

Daily calls turned into long nights of conversation.
Text messages turned into promises.
Missed moments turned into planned trips.

I flew to Albuquerque once or twice a month just to be with him.
We were no longer hiding.
We were no longer guessing.

We were official.

And for the first time in a long time...
I felt light.
I felt sure.
I felt chosen.

Meeting His Children

Then came a moment that changed everything.

Marcus introduced me to his kids.

I was terrified.

Not of their judgment—
but of the weight of what that introduction meant.

They were his world.
His heart.
His reason for living.

And now...
I was being brought into that sacred space.

The first time we met, they looked at me with curiosity.
Then with smiles.
Then with warmth.

Before I even realized it, they were running toward me, hugging me,
asking me questions, laughing with me.

And in that moment, something inside me broke and healed at the
same time.

For the first time...
I felt like I truly belonged.

Holidays That Felt Like Home

Christmas came.

And instead of loneliness...
there were lights.
Laughter.
Kids running around the house.
Marcus cooking in the kitchen.
My name being called with excitement.

Every summer, they waited for me.
Every Christmas, they looked for me.

"Is Kim coming?" they would ask.

And I always did.

I wasn't just visiting anymore.

I was becoming part of their life.

Meeting His Mother

Then came his mother.

I was nervous the entire drive.

What if she didn't accept me?
What if she saw me as a mistake?
What if she only tolerated me for her son?

But when I met her…

She was warm.
Gentle.
Kind.

She asked about my life.
My work.
My family.

We talked like two women trying to understand each other.

And for the first time in my life…
I felt what it meant to be welcomed without hesitation.

What I Had Always Wanted

In Marcus' world, I was not a secret.
Not a fantasy.
Not a phase.

I was:

- His partner

- His love

- A part of his family

- A presence in his children's lives

- A woman his mother welcomed

And as I stood there—
watching his children laugh,
hearing his mother speak kindly to me,
feeling Marcus' hand in mine—

I realized something painful and beautiful at the same time:

This... this was everything I had ever asked for.

To belong.
To be accepted.
To be loved without conditions.
To feel chosen not just in words—but in life.

CHAPTER THIRTY:

THE DISTANCE THAT ALMOST TORE US APART

My days in the United States were numbered.

My teaching contract was almost over, and as part of my program, I was required to return to the Philippines. Whether I was ready or not, I had to leave.

So, I started applying to other countries.

And just like always...
I got hired.

But this time, there was no excitement.
No celebration.
No victory.

Because my heart was no longer searching for a place to belong.

My heart already belonged here.
With Marcus.

But Marcus and I were never the type to rush into conversations about forever.
He came from a failed marriage, and I understood his fear.

So after that one difficult conversation about marriage months ago, I stopped bringing it up.

Not because I didn't want forever with him—
but because I was afraid to hope again.

Marcus knew about my situation.
He knew my visa was ending.
He knew I was preparing to leave.

But I didn't know what he planned.

All I knew was that the clock was ticking.

Two years.

Two years away from him.
Two years of different time zones.
Two years of loving through screens.
Two years of missing his face beside me every morning.

To me...
two years felt like a slow death.

But I was afraid to ask him what he thought.
Afraid of hearing the wrong answer.
Afraid of losing him even before leaving.

The Night Everything Changed

One quiet evening, the world finally forced the conversation.

We were sitting beside each other—
no music,
no distractions,
just silence between two people who both knew something was about to change.

I took a deep breath.

"Marcus... I got accepted to teach in another country," I said softly.
"I have to leave. It's part of my program."

He didn't speak right away.

Instead, he reached for my hand and held it tight.

Then he looked at me and asked the question that made my knees weak:

"If you truly love me... would you choose me over all of that?"

I didn't know how to answer.

My whole life had been built on survival.
On choosing opportunity over comfort.
On choosing growth over attachment.

And now…
for the first time, someone was asking me to choose **love**.

Before I could speak, Marcus stood up and walked toward the drawer near his desk.

He came back holding a **brown envelope**.

"What's that?" I asked.

"Open it."

My hands trembled as I pulled the papers out.

And then I saw it.

Official divorce papers.
Stamped.
Signed.
Final.

His marriage was legally over.

My heart started pounding so loudly I thought I might faint.

In that quiet room—
no crowd,
no spotlight,
no audience—

Marcus took a deep breath…

and said the words that changed my life:

"Will you marry me?"

The Choice I Had Been Praying For

No grand restaurant.
No champagne.
No photographers.
No scripted perfection.

Just two people in a quiet room,
afraid of losing each other.

"I can't imagine waking up without you beside me," he said.
"I can't accept the idea of you being a thousand miles away for two
years.
I fear that if you go… I might lose you forever."

That night, I finally understood something:

Love doesn't need a stage to be real.
It just needs truth.

I couldn't find the right words.

My voice broke as I whispered—

"Yes. I will."

We hugged like two people who had almost lost each other.
We kissed like two people who had waited too long to stop running.

That night…
I wasn't chosen because of fantasy.
I wasn't chosen because of pity.
I wasn't chosen because of circumstance.

I was chosen because I was loved.

And for the first time in my life—
the person I loved most…

chose me back.

CHAPTER THIRTY-ONE:

THE LOVE THAT FINALLY STAYED

Letting go of Fernando was not as loud as our wedding had been.

There were no guests.
No camera flashes.
No music swelling in the background.

Just two people sitting across from each other—
finally brave enough to stop pretending.

My hands were shaking when I told him about Marcus.
About the proposal.
About the life I was choosing this time—not out of fear, not out of
pressure, but out of truth.

Fernando listened.

No interruptions.
No anger.
No accusations.

When I finished, he exhaled slowly and said the words I never
expected to hear:

"It's okay, Kim. I want you to be happy."

There was no bitterness in his voice.
No hatred.
Only quiet surrender.

In that moment, I realized—
we were never meant to destroy each other.
We were only meant to teach each other how to let go.

We agreed to file for divorce.

And just like our fast wedding,
our marriage ended just as quickly.

One month.

That was all it took to legally close a chapter
that the heart had already abandoned long ago.

Before I walked away for the last time, I hugged Fernando.

A long hug.
Not of lovers—
but of two people who once tried to save each other
with the wrong kind of love.

Then I bent down and kissed our daughter goodbye.

Mulan.
Our dog.
The only pure soul our marriage had ever known.

I whispered, "Be good, ha?"

And with that, I walked out of a life
that was never meant to last.

A Wedding Without Fear

Marcus and I made plans.

Not for a grand wedding.
Not for a fairy-tale spectacle.
Not for validation in the eyes of the world.

I had already lived that lie.

This time, all I wanted was something quiet.
Simple.
Certain.

But life, as always, tried to test us again.

US immigration rules tightened.
Travel became uncertain.
Once more, fear knocked on my door.

And then—without hesitation,
without complaints,
without waiting for a safer time—

Marcus drove all the way to Las Vegas just to marry me.

I didn't beg.
I didn't demand.
I didn't even expect it.

He chose it.

And in that choice, I knew:

This is love.
Not the loud kind.
Not the desperate kind.
But the kind that moves—
the kind that sacrifices—
the kind that doesn't calculate the cost.

Only a few of our closest friends were there.
Marcus told his mom.
He told his children.

With the help of my chosen family,
the wedding happened.

No spotlight.

Just truth.

The Bride With No Doubts

My gown wasn't expensive.

But for the first time in my life—
my heart was rich.

No trembling from fear.
No shaking from doubt.

Only the soft, sacred trembling
of someone who finally knows
she is standing in the right place.

As I walked toward Marcus,
the world went quiet.

All the noise of my past fell away—
the hunger,
the rejection,
the shame,
the versions of me that had begged to be chosen.

All that remained
was the man waiting for me
without reservations,
without conditions,
without running.

We exchanged our rings.
We spoke our vows.

And when he kissed me…

It did not feel like an ending.

It felt like **arrival**.

The Life I Chose

Marcus took me back with him to Albuquerque.

And for the first time in my life—
I came home to a home
that did not feel temporary.

We built a life together.
We fought.
We healed.
We learned how to love without fear.

And six years later…

We are still here.

Not perfect.
Not untouched by storms.
But stronger.
Wiser.
Still choosing each other—every single day.

This is the life I once prayed for in secret.
This is the love I once begged for in tears.
This is the woman I once dreamed of becoming
while standing in places that did not see my worth.

I am happy.
I am content.
And this—
this is the version of **Maria Kim**
I fought so hard to become.

And at last…

She is finally living.

EPILOGUE:

THE WAR AFTER THE PEACE

Just when I thought the storms of my life had finally calmed...
another battlefield opened.

Not in classrooms.
Not in relationships.
Not in marriages.

But on a phone screen.

On TikTok.

While I was quietly fixing my life, healing my heart, and building my
marriage, a new fight was waiting for me—louder, crueler, and
watched by thousands of strangers.

I was judged.
I was mocked.
I was misunderstood.
Looked down on because I was once poor.
Because I was loud.
Because I was visible.
Because I refused to stay silent.

People who didn't know my story suddenly had opinions about my
worth.

Friends turned into enemies.
Enemies turned into unexpected family.

Ate Kim.
Sky.

The people who were once my loudest critics later became some of
my closest allies. Life has a strange way of flipping the script when
you least expect it.

And in the middle of all that chaos, I found people who never left.

Gretchen.
Ivy.
Team California.
LDF.
Team Daga.

They stood beside me when it was easiest to walk away.
When the comments were cruel.
When the lies were loud.
When the pressure was unbearable.

That whole circus was fun…
but it was also exhausting.
Entertaining…
but painful.
Empowering…
but dangerous.

And somehow, through the noise, I learned even more about myself.

That healing doesn't mean the battles stop.
It just means you learn how to fight smarter.
Stronger.
With your head high.

This book told the story of how I survived life, love, loss, and transformation.

The next one…
will tell the story of how I survived the world watching me break—and rise—again.

Because sometimes, the loudest wars happen
after you finally find your peace.

To be continued…

Becoming Maria Kim

A Love Letter to the Ones Who Never Left

This book carries my story —
but it does not belong to me alone.

This story exists because I did not survive life by myself.

To my **Mama and Papa** —
thank you for the sacrifices you made when we had nothing but faith
and hope.
Your love may not always have been perfect, but it was always the
foundation I stood on.

To my **siblings, Florame and Kevin** —
thank you for being my strength in silence, my comfort in distance,
and my reminder of where I came from.

To my **bestfriend, Henry** —
thank you for seeing me long before the world did.
For staying when it was easier to walk away.
For loving me when I barely knew how to love myself.

To my **online families who became my real-life shelter** —
Team Gorgeous, Team California, Team LDF —
you were never just names on a screen.
You became my comfort, my laughter, my defense, and my home.

To the women who became my **mother's here in the US** —
Ate Jean, Ate Inday Rosing, Madam Arga, and Mommy Glen —
you filled the spaces where homesickness once lived.
You fed me, scolded me, prayed for me, protected me, and loved me
like your own.

To my **sponsors and angels who helped carry my dreams** —
Ma'am Wheng, Russel, and the many others whose kindness never
asked for anything in return —
you believed in my future when my present was still uncertain.

And to the **online strangers who became my family** —
who defended me, lifted me, supported me, prayed for me, and held my hands through a screen —
thank you for proving that community can be built even in the most unexpected places.

To everyone who stayed when I was loud, broken, healing, rising, and becoming —
this life I now live is also yours.

This book is not just a story of becoming **Maria Kim**.
It is a story of how **love — in all its forms — saved me**.

And if you finished this book carrying even a little more hope than when you started it,
then every pain I survived had a purpose.

This is not the end.

This is just the beginning.

With all my love,
Maria Kim